T0021474

DISFIGURED

ON FAIRY TALES, DISABILITY, AND MAKING SPACE

AMANDA LEDUC

COACH HOUSE BOOKS, TORONTO

copyright © Amanda Leduc, 2020

first edition

Published with the generous assistance of the Canada Council for the Arts and the Ontario Arts Council. Coach House Books also gratefully acknowledges the support of the Government of Canada through the Canada Book Fund and the Government of Ontario through the Ontario Book Publishing Tax Credit.

LIBRARY AND ARCHIVES CANADA CATALOGUING IN PUBLICATION

Title: Disfigured : on fairy tales, disability, and making space / Amanda Leduc.
Names: Leduc, Amanda, author.
Series: Exploded views.
Description: Series statement: Exploded views
Identifiers: Canadiana (print) 2019014453X | Canadiana (ebook) 20190144564 | ISBN 9781552453957 (softcover) | ISBN 9781770566057 (PDF) | ISBN 9781770566040 (EPUB)
Subjects: LCSH: Fairy tales—History and criticism. | LCSH: Disabilities in literature. | LCSH: People with disabilities in literature.
Classification: LCC PN3437 .L43 2020 | DDC 398/.3561—dc23

Disfigured is available as an ebook: ISBN 978 1 77056 604 0 (EPUB), ISBN 978 1 77056 605 7 (PDF).

Purchase of the print version of this book entitles you to a free digital copy. To claim your ebook of this title, please email sales@chbooks.com with proof of purchase. (Coach House Books reserves the right to terminate the free download offer at any time.)

For Dorothy, who showed me the path into the woods;

*For Jael, who helped me to see that I was brave enough
to follow it;*

*And for all of my disabled brothers and sisters, who
held my hands so that I did not go down the path alone.*

No one ever sees Sophocles' play as a drama about
a cripple and a blind man fighting over Thebes.
– Tobin Siebers

Your once-silken voice will desert you, your legs
will make every step on land a torture.
There will come a time when you miss
the seaweed and seals, your old ways,
your old body. Now fit for neither land
nor sea, your sacrifice long in the past now.
Comb your hair, which keeps growing,
though you've lost your prince.
You know the time is coming
where you'll pay the price
for your short time in the sun.
– Jeannine Hall Gailey

Introduction

Rather appropriately, the idea for this book came to me while I was in the forest. In the summer of 2018 I had the extraordinary good fortune to participate in a three-week writing retreat at Hedgebrook Farm, on Whidbey Island off the coast of Seattle. I was working on a novel, and after a particularly challenging day took myself out to the woods to try and find some solace. There was a walking stick at the front door of my cottage, and I took it without thinking, then set off toward the back of the property. Somewhere at the far north end of the farm was a blackberry bush, and I was eager to reach it and fill my hands with berries.

As I walked, I thought idly about how much easier going it was with the walking stick – an inanimate companion to help me along through all of the forest's dips and swells and hollows. It was helpful even on the paved ground closer to my residence. With the walking stick in my hand, I felt sure of myself, confident. It balanced my weight as I shifted from foot to foot in a way that was thrillingly surprising.

Does this mean I should use a cane in regular life? I wondered as I made my way to the blackberries. *Would it be helpful? How would that change the way I move through the world?*

I don't use a cane in my day-to-day. I have mild cerebral palsy and spastic hemiplegia, and though I walk with a visible limp, my balance has been good enough, for my first three and a half decades, to allow me to walk unaided.

But I do stare at the ground when I walk, a fact that I was completely unaware of until a chiropodist pointed it out at an appointment when I was twenty-seven. It took a few more years for me to realize that I stare at the ground because the ground is full of danger – unpredictable and capricious, with gaps between concrete blocks, uneven bricks, cracks in the sidewalk. If I do not pay attention to where my feet are all the time, it's pretty much guaranteed that I will fall at some point in my walking.

A cane, I thought, would probably be helpful.

For many of us with physical disabilities, the forest is often a dangerous place to be. There's no hope of taking a wheelchair into the trees unless there's a clearly marked and flattened path; it can be difficult to navigate a forest even with a guide dog at your side. I'd wager that the forest presents trouble perhaps even for those whose disabilities are often deemed invisible – it can be a dark place, filled with all manner of smells and sensory onslaughts, a place where even the able-bodied can lose themselves.

A princess in a wheelchair would have trouble finding those blackberries, I thought as I crept through the bushes. And then I stopped, briefly, and smiled. A princess in a wheelchair? *Whoever heard of such a thing?*

But by the time I reached the blackberry bush, that unknown princess in her wheelchair was all I could think about. That princess, and the seven dwarfs who helped Snow White, and Rumpelstiltskin, and the ugliness of the Beast in 'Beauty and the Beast,' the evil queen in 'Snow White' who transforms herself into a hunchbacked old woman, the prince who goes blind after the witch casts Rapunzel from her tower, the princess who falls into a long, enchanted sleep. The witch with the crutch in 'Hansel and Gretel,' the stepsisters who get their eyes plucked out by doves in 'Aschenputtel' – the Brothers Grimm version of 'Cinderella' – and all the ugly princes and princesses who gain the throne by their cunning and then are made or revealed to be beautiful after all.

And suddenly I was no longer alone in the forest; suddenly I was thinking about these connections, disability and fairy tales, how *obvious*, how had I not considered these things before?

This needed to be an essay, I thought. But no doubt it was already an essay; no doubt the link between fairy tales and disability had been written about a million times before. There was *so much* in there that one could write about. People far smarter than I had no doubt already done it, and done it well. I filled my soul with blackberries and went back to my cottage. I went back to working on the novel.

I also kept thinking about that long stretch of moments in the forest. Disability and fairy tales. Disability *in* fairy tales. When I got home I did some research and found surprisingly little on the topic; sure that I was missing something, I dug a little harder. My digging brought me Ann Schmiesing and her wonderful book *Disability, Deformity, and Disease in the Grimms' Fairy Tales*. My digging brought me to Sharon Snyder and David T. Mitchell and their work on narrative prosthesis, to the work of disability-studies scholar Tobin Siebers, to the fantastic breadth of scholarship afforded by Jack Zipes.

And it brought me, again, to the fairy tales. So many darker versions of the Disney stories that I'd known as a child – and so many darker moments in the Disney stories, too. Why was Scar, the villain of *The Lion King*, known only by the mark that slashed his face? Why did the depiction of the 'hunchback'

Quasimodo make my skin crawl? Why hadn't I ever thought of *The Little Mermaid*'s Ariel in those moments just after she'd arrived on land with legs and seen myself in her unsteady posture and stumbling?

Why, in all of these stories about someone who wants to be something or someone else, was it always the individual who needed to change, and never the world?

Disfigured is my attempt at unravelling some of the more well-known Western fairy-tale archetypes in light of a disability rights framework. In order to understand how we move on from the damage that these archetypes can do, we first need to understand what put them in place – why the disfigured body has historically been seen as less than whole; why fairy tales, narratives so often associated with seeming empowerment, have provided a breeding ground for anti-disability narrative; and how the allure and the potency of these stories has continued to influence the perceptions of disability today. To reclaim disability narrative in storytelling, we need to understand *why* stories like fairy tales have been fascinated with it right from the very beginning, and how the stories we tell have maligned difference – and disability – in order to make sense of it in the world.

A few notes. As someone who grew up on Western fairy tales and their various interpretations, it is my intention to stay in my lane, as it were, and focus the majority of this book on fairy tales and several pop culture hero narratives that are familiar to a Western audience. While I make mention of several tales from other cultures in an effort to show the pervasiveness of certain archetypes, the bulk of this book remains focused on Western stories and several modern interpretations that stem from predominantly European frameworks. I very much hope this book can contribute to the conversations around disability in fairy tales from other cultures, and look forward to continued learning around this.

It's also important to note that this book is not a work of fairy-tale scholarship. My intention is to approach fairy tales from the perspective of someone who has loved them but operated with what amounts to a layperson's knowledge of the tales throughout most of her life. I am interested specifically in where the fairy-tale narrative and its archetypes intersect with disability representation, and have used that framework to guide the book. As such, my interpretations of several tales and their relationships to disability may at times seem to group certain tales together that have traditionally been considered very different from one another (for example, in the sections on the tales of the Brothers Grimm and Hans Christian Andersen's 'The Little Mermaid').

Nor is this book meant to be a work of disability scholarship. I am a physically disabled woman who also deals with a major depressive disorder, and while I use my own experience to explore fairy tales and their cultural impact in the world, it is not my intention here to speak for the field of disability studies or for all disabled people, or for all those who likewise deal with their own mental health challenges on a regular basis. Disability is not a monolith – every disabled person's experience in the world is different, and the way that we all navigate the world is likewise varied and complex.

I also think it's important to note that my experience as a white disabled woman makes my ability to comment on multiple marginalizations within the disabled community necessarily limited. We need to make space for, pay attention to, and elevate the stories of disabled people from IBPOC (Indigenous, Black, and People of Colour) communities. The question of how the Western fairy-tale framework has contributed to the colonialist and capitalist structures that continue to disenfranchise IBPOC disabled communities today is one that all white disabled people should be asking, no matter the intersections within our own communities, and I hope that the questions posed in this book can help to spark further conversations around how fairy tales have impacted and hurt disabled IBPOC communities in particular. It is my hope this book can speak to people in whatever way they need, and that in telling my own particular story and exploring the way disability operates in some of the Western world's best-known fairy tales, this book can help further the conversation around disability representation in the stories we tell in our modern world.

Interspersed throughout *Disfigured* are doctor's notes from the initial consultation that my parents had with the neurosurgeon who operated on me when I was four. I have included excerpts from these notes because understanding the story my parents were told about my disability – and, indeed, the story my doctors told themselves about it – has been crucial to my own understanding of how my disability operates in my life today. In sharing my doctor's words here, my aim is to take back the narrative. However, I want to stress that medical records are not something disabled people should be expected to share as a part of our stories, and while I have been incredibly fortunate – and privileged – in my experience with the medical world, I am well aware that this is not the case for many.

I spoke with many disabled individuals over the course of writing *Disfigured*, and as a general rule use identity-first language throughout the text, unless otherwise requested. Identity-first language ('disabled person') holds that the disabled identity is an important part of what makes someone a person in the first place, inextricably bound up with how someone navigates the world. Person-first language, by contrast, argues that an individual must be seen as a person first and someone with a disability second ('person with a disability'). The general consensus among disability activists is that person-first language, while well-meaning, separates disability from identity and thus continues to malign disability and perpetuate the idea that it is a negative thing.

The disabilities and pronouns of every individual cited in this book have been expressed according to their wishes.

I am grateful to all of those who chose to share their time and expertise with me. It is my fervent hope that the explorations in this book do everybody justice.

1

The Child Whose Head Was Bathed in Darkness

It begins, as all fairy tales do, with a problem. Once upon a time, a woodcutter and his wife lived alone and had no children. Once upon a time, a wealthy man's wife died and he was lonely, so he married another woman who was cruel to his child. Once upon a time, a mermaid, looking out beyond the sea, longed to find herself walking on land.

In this case, a mother and father have a seventeen-month-old daughter who has not yet learned to walk. This is not always a problem – some children walk sooner, others take their time – but these parents are worried. They read the literature on standard milestones and ask questions of the doctors, who tell them not to worry. They whisper the same thing to themselves and each other at night: *Don't worry. Everything will be okay.*

They've already lost a child – another daughter, dark-haired and silent, who came into the world already dead. It happened a year and a half before their second daughter was born. Her ashes sit in a little grey box on their bedroom closet shelf. They are terrified but also filled with hope.

Sometimes it can take a while, they remind themselves. *Every child is different.* Their second daughter's other milestones are fine. She laughs, she cries, she crawled with no trouble. She eats anything and everything they put in front of her.

(*Such a good little eater*, her grandfather says. Years later, it will be their longest-running family joke.)

When she does take her first steps, just before turning two, they are overjoyed but still worried. Their daughter's right foot turns inward, so that her right leg collapses against the left. She doesn't drag it, not exactly, but the way she walks doesn't look quite right. There are no mentions of this in their baby information books, no pictures of a leg that slants *just so*. They take her to the doctor, who agrees that something doesn't look the way it should.

More than this, though: the doctor trusts them, believes them, understands the dark river of uncertainty that flows deep within a parent.

'I listen to the mothers,' she tells them. 'They always know.'

She refers them to a neurologist, who sends them to another city an hour's drive away, so that doctors can put the girl into a machine and look at her brain.

Fairy tales, as we understand them in the modern Western world, have a rich and varied history. The *Oxford Companion to Fairy Tales* defines them as 'narratives of magic and fantasy, which are understood to be fictional.' The specific term *fairy tale* comes to us from the 1697 publication of the French noblewoman Marie-Catherine d'Aulnoy's *Les contes des fées*, but fairy tales existed in both oral and written form much earlier than this. In fact, many such tales were oral in nature long before they were written down, which means the form is, in its power to keep shape over thousands of years, stronger than most other stories we tell – and yet, subject to the whims of oral retelling, also that much more delicate.

Some fairy tales are a subclass of the *folk tale*, a term that has grown to be quite wide-ranging and references a body of work that encompasses the stories, tales, and myths and legends of a particular culture. (While the lines can sometimes blur, the folklorist William Bascom has noted that folklorists tend to distinguish myths and legends from fairy tales in terms of the attitudes that people hold toward them. Myths, according to the scholar Elliott Oring, 'are seen as both sacred and true,' while legends focus on a single, miraculous episode in a story. Fairy tales, by contrast, are known to be magical and fictional right from beginning to end.)

Still other fairy tales come to us not from the oral tradition but are original creations with known authors. There are fairy-tale elements in *The Golden Ass*, the only surviving novel from Greek antiquity; there are elements of fairy tale in 'Bel and the Dragon,' which appears in the book of Daniel in the Old Testament and is usually dated to the fifth or sixth century BCE. Hans Christian Andersen wrote original fairy tales, as did Lewis Carroll and Edith Nesbit. *Peter Pan*, by J. M. Barrie, brought fairy-tale elements into a book treasured by children and adults alike, as did L. Frank Baum, the writer of *The Wonderful Wizard of Oz*.

Though the term *fairy tale* as we understand it in Western culture generally applies to the European tales, the umbrella of *folk tale* encompasses stories told all over the world. In many cases, versions of classic European fairy tales have similar counterparts in other countries, some stories preceding their European counterparts by centuries, if not more. Stories like 'Jack and the Beanstalk,' 'Beauty and the Beast,' and 'Rumpelstiltskin,' in their varying forms around the world, have had their origins traced to over four thousand years ago.

Essentially, we started telling ourselves stories pretty much as soon as we could speak. While fairy tale as a genre is a relatively recent development, it's a kind of story that has existed in various ways since the beginning of time.

Specifically, we have used this storytelling form to illustrate that which is different; whether that difference is disfigurement or social exclusion, fairy tales often centre in some way on protagonists who are set apart from the rest of the world.

'The purpose of stories,' says the scholar David T. Mitchell, 'is to explain that which has stepped out of line. Understanding differences in people is one of the first things that propels the act of storytelling into existence.'

It is through stories that we give shape to and understand the world – and historically, it has been through stories that we've first given shape to difference. Without the capacity of science to understand that which doesn't fit in line, it only makes sense that stories are the first things to make that space.

I am three years old when my parents take me to a hospital in London, Ontario, for a CT scan. I don't remember much of this – I might remember feeling closed in by the gigantic, whirring CT machine, but there were other CT scans that came in later years, so it's likely I remember those ones instead. It is my parents who hold these memories: the drive to this other city almost two hours away, the creeping sense of dread as they sat in the car, the small attempts at making conversation. Maybe I fell asleep in the car on the way there – it's likely that I did. I still fall asleep in cars, all these years later.

I am three years old and playing around on the floor when the neurologist calls my mother with the results and tells her there is empty space where parts of my brain should be. The scans show a dark mass in the centre of my cerebrum, nestled between the left hemisphere and the right.

'There should be muscle,' the neurologist says, 'and there's nothing.'

My mother starts to cry. I reach for her, confused.

But she knows who I am, my mother thinks. *She doesn't look like she doesn't have a brain. How does any of that make sense?*

The neurologist recommends surgery; she recommends another doctor. We go for a consultation. My parents do not like him.

'He was a young doctor,' my mother tells me now. 'You could tell that he really didn't know what to do, that he was guessing.' In desperation, my mother turns to her cousin, a cardiac nurse. Her cousin asks around and comes back to them with a name: Dr. Humphreys, who works at the Hospital for Sick Children in Toronto. This hospital sits another hour or so away from my home city, in the opposite direction.

If the doctor had asked them, my parents would have gone into the forest and found a hazel branch, then planted it outside the front door and waited for rain. They would have killed a fatted calf and spread the blood over the door, or taken me to a witch who lived in the woods and asked for a potion to mix into my food. They would have met an old man at the door of their house and, knowing instinctively that he was the Devil in disguise, promised him the riches of their home and land in exchange for my health. They would have done, they will do, anything to make sure their little girl stays safe and whole. They cannot imagine what life would be like otherwise.

We tell ourselves stories in order to live, Joan Didion says.

They take me to the hospital, they fold their hands and pray.

Unlike both legends and myths, fairy tales are generally seen as not being grounded in any kind of historical truth. Their primary purpose is often moralistic; fairy tales exist to teach us things, to tell us something about a part of the world that has, in some way, been misunderstood. In German folklore they are known as *Märchen*, or *wonder stories*. These tales rarely contain fairies, but all contain some element of the wondrous: goose girls who become princesses, heroes who kill dragons, queens who call on magic to bring them a child.

In Europe, the genre as a literary form took shape during the Renaissance, with the collected works of Italian writers such as Giovan Francesco Straparola (*The Pleasant Nights*) and Giambattista Basile (*The Pentamerone*, of which 'Sun, Moon, and Talia' is the first written iteration of 'Sleeping Beauty') making space for the later tales of Charles Perrault (France) and the Brothers Grimm (Germany).

In the seventeenth century, when Madame d'Aulnoy began writing her tales in France, the literary fairy tale became fashionable as a pastime among aristocratic women, in salons where the stories were told and retold among different groups. Here is where we can begin to see the effect of social and cultural change on the stories; the focus of fairy tales shifted to highlight particular morals and etiquette, all of them told with grand oratorial panache that, in turn, began to influence the shape and structure of literary language and style.

The collected fairy tales of the Brothers Grimm, published in Germany as *Kinder- und Hausmärchen* ('Children's and Household Tales'), arguably the most famous example of European oral fairy tales to be bundled in written form, were, in fact, started as a way of countering this rise in high-minded 'literary' style. The Brothers Grimm were intent on preserving the – as they saw it – natural poetry (*'Naturpoesie'*) inherent to German folk tales and stories, which they felt was at its truest form among the peasant class, and thus in danger of disappearing as the world slowly turned toward the preservation of literary forms in books and other publications. Early introductions to the Grimms' first editions of the tales praised the 'robust' and 'healthy' nature of many of those who shared stories with the Grimms – a nature the brothers saw as crucial to the storytelling. In the same way that industrialization and the move to urban centres was beginning to threaten the German peasant way of life, so too did the Grimms see the advent of literary culture as a threat to the traditions of storytelling they'd known all their lives.

'There is thus a parallel,' says literature scholar Ann Schmiesing, 'between the precariousness of the human condition and the precariousness of the orally transmitted fairy tale … the fairy tale cannot survive unless it is orally transmitted and listened to or written down or read.'

One major irony here is that Wilhelm and Jacob Grimm collected a significant number of their tales from aristocratic women and not, in fact, from the peasant class. In the original edition of the *Kinder und Hausmärchen* (henceforth abbreviated as the *KHM*), Jacob Grimm, in his appendices, praised the storytelling of one Dorothea Viehmann in particular – a 'robust, healthy individual, with a large propensity for remembering tales and a set of clear bright eyes that saw right into your soul.' Viehmann was in fact middle class – an innkeeper's widow, a woman in her fifties with several children she had sole responsibility for feeding. She died of illness after the second edition of the *KHM* came out.

Nevertheless, the work of the Brothers Grimm had a lasting effect throughout Europe, prompting collectors and folklorists in other countries to collect and preserve their own stories, feeding the nationalism and the penchant for cultural tales that was sweeping the continent. The decision to title their work 'Children's and Household Tales' had the similarly wide-reaching effect of shaping the fairy-tale genre more specifically for younger eyes across many countries for centuries.

As we will see, subsequent retellings of the fairy tales – think Disney and its princesses – pushed this child-friendly focus even further, removing many of the original elements in stories like 'Rapunzel' and 'Cinderella' (Rapunzel's pregnancy in the tower, the stepsisters' self-mutilation in pursuit of Cinderella's glass slipper) in favour of making the tales brighter, both visually, in the case of Disney, and in content. While the twentieth century also saw a discreet pull away from the staunchly religious overtones of the Brothers Grimm, the sharpened focus on the bright and happy ending was its own kind of moralizing – an attempt to impose order over chaos, to replace the stern and sometimes arbitrary hand of God with a benevolent universe in which all good things come to those who merit them. While there were plenty of tales in the KHM and in other collections that did not, in fact, end happily, many of the stories that have survived and been retold the most – the ones we keep coming back to – are those with the happy endings. The arc of the moral universe now bends toward the good in all of these old stories that we tell.

Happy endings come to all, one way or another.

At least, they do if you deserve them.

A biopsy of the brain mass confirms that it isn't a *tumour* – instead it's a cyst, which sounds a little bit better than tumour but is still terrifying. It is unusual, the doctor tells my parents, to see cysts where mine is growing, right in the centre of the brain.

Cerebral Palsy. A neurological disorder that affects movement, motor skills, and muscle tone. Dr. Humphreys is different from the other doctor who made my mother so nervous – he is older, warmer, more confident – so when he delivers these words to her, they aren't quite as terrifying as she expected them to be. Years later I will discover that his first name is Robin, which suits him in a way I can't articulate, a man who is confident and serious but still a child in all the ways that matter. He is playful and kind, like a wise and gentle grandpa. If he turned into an animal, it makes sense that this animal would be a red-breasted bird.

'The cyst is like a ball of water on the brain,' he says. 'We'll put in a shunt to drain it out.'

A vp shunt, to be specific. A device that's usually placed in the ventricles of the brain to treat hydrocephalus. I won't know how to say the word itself until almost a decade has passed. *Vee-pee, Vee-pee, Vee-pee. Ventriculoperitoneal.* The full word trips over my tongue like *Rumpelstiltskin*.

To insert the shunt, the surgeons shave the left half of my head and open my skull flap. They slide the shunt through the main left ventricle, then feed the long plastic tubing of the shunt down past my organs, to rest in a silvery coil in my abdomen. As I grow, inch by inch, the silvery coil will unfurl and stretch out with me. ('If she grows taller than six foot three,' the surgeon later jokes to my parents, 'she's in trouble.') The shunt will drain the cerebrospinal fluid that's collecting in the cyst, then filter it down to my intestines, where it will collect in my urine and pass out of my body. Problem solved, like magic.

My parents are weeping and grateful, cautious but still scared. (*Why did they only shave half of her head?* my mother thinks but doesn't say.) I stay in the hospital for observation.

Soon it becomes clear that the shunt isn't working. (Worry is a dark river that has no end.) Most cysts are made of water – mine, as it turns out, is more gelatinous. It must be sliced out, and so I go back into surgery. This time they shave the other half of my head, too, and slice into the mass. The cyst is removed, sliver by sliver. My mother, who is seven months pregnant with my brother, cradles her belly as she and my father sit in the waiting room.

The surgery is successful – as successful as it can be. The doctors get almost all of the cyst, save for the little bits grafted closest to the brain tissue. Dr. Humphreys doesn't think they'll grow back.

'We'll see her every year in checkup, just to be sure.'

When my parents come in to see me after the surgery, I'm bleary-eyed but awake.

'Do you know who I am?' my mother asks, nervously.

I look at her, confused by the strange questions of adults in the way that only a four-year-old can be. 'Yes,' I say. 'Don't you?'

She wants to laugh, or cry, but does neither. Instead she sits gingerly on the bed and hugs me, careful of the bandages around my head. I look so tiny, swimming in the bed, swimming in my hospital gown.

As the days go by, I recover, but grumpily. My mother spends her nights at the hotel across the street from the hospital, weeping alone in the shower. She doesn't believe in fairy tales, but this is another dark river, a whisper, a warning. Maybe something came into that operating room and took me away, then left another girl in my place. 'There's something wrong,' she begs the nurses. 'That isn't the little girl I know.'

But it is, and I am – I'm just *grumpy*. I don't like being in the hospital. I hate how the bandage itches on my head. I hate that the nurse has to help me take my bath. I hate the food, I hate how I'm supposed to play with the other children in the playroom, I hate the fact that the nurses come in to take my temperature every few hours at night. I hate the beep of the thermometer, the deep red of the digital numbers. I hate the cold feel of the metal under my tongue. I hate the nurses' brisk cheerfulness when I try to refuse.

If you don't open your mouth for the thermometer, I'll have to take your temperature from your bum!

I hate that my favourite nurse, Margaret, tells me not to cry in front of my mother when I see her next. *Of course* I want to be strong for my mother. *Of course* I don't want to let her down.

I burst into tears as soon as I see her, and I hate that even more.

Soon, though, we leave the hospital. It's April. I'm home for the rest of my junior kindergarten year. My hair grows back, slowly. One day, at the playground, a girl asks, *Mummy, why is that little boy wearing a dress?* and I run crying to my mother.

My right foot still turns inward, and so in a year's time there is another surgery, this one to lengthen the tendons in my foot and turn it to face outward — properly, *normally*. I wear a cast for six weeks and have a taxi that drives me to school, and a wheelchair that other kids in my class are excited to push me around in until the novelty wears off.

When the cast comes off, I have a limp. I can walk, but I do not walk normally. My hips are uneven. The lengthened tendons can only do so much — my right foot is misshapen and scarred. I have to wear special shoes, and the right shoe is larger than the left. It is barely noticeable, if at all, but even at five and six years old, it's all I can see.

Almost all fairy tales involve some kind of quest, whether it's physical – as in the case of the Grimms' 'Two Travellers,' where the tailor and the butcher are sent on a quest by a witch in order to find and marry a princess – or spiritual, as in the case of the Grimms' 'The Maiden Without Hands,' where the titular character wanders alone through the woods with her severed hands tied to her back. People are sent out into the world to *learn something*, to complete a series of tasks, gather a series of objects, in order to overcome their struggles and return triumphant to their lives. Do this, do that, and all will be okay.

In the Norwegian version of the fairy tale 'East of the Sun and West of the Moon,' the main character must journey to the castle where her husband is held captive and save him from a troll princess; in Hans Christian Andersen's 'The Little Mermaid,' the mermaid must kill her beloved prince in order to regain her voice and return triumphant to the sea.

Quests appear in literature and oral tradition as far back as Gilgamesh; they resonate through cultures spread over the world. In one tale of Anansi the spider, the beloved African folk hero, Anansi must journey and bring back Onini the python, Osebo the leopard, and the Mboro hornets so Nyame, the Sky-God, will release stories into the world.

Anansi captures the animals and releases the stories; the tailor outwits the butcher and marries the princess; the maiden in 'The Maiden Without Hands' finds benevolent strangers who help her, and her hands grow back as a reward for her faith. Each quest in every fairy tale comes to some kind of conclusion. Even the Little Mermaid, who kills herself at the end of the original story, is promised the eternal happy ending of heaven.

I am the happy ending my parents were hoping for, and also, for myself, somehow not. The fact that I have survived is the best of outcomes – the triumphant return home from a quest far away, the reward for tasks completed and done in perfect, exacting manner. My parents have listened to the doctors and the gurus and garnered all the advice from wise men and women that they can. My brain has been opened and the offending particles removed, a process that is entirely scientific and also entirely magical. Everything is terrifying and then everything is okay. But the realities of this new, post-surgery life are a different matter altogether.

Life is always different from the happy endings we see in the fairy tales we're exposed to in books and on screens. We know this instinctively, and yet the assumptions and preconceptions we have as a result of these oldest of stories continue to permeate so many aspects of Western culture today.

I *knew*, growing up, that my life as a disabled child was just as valuable as that of any other girl. But I did not know – and sometimes still don't – how to fit physically into that 'valuable' space. I was not the girl who was graceful in dance class, even though I wanted to be; I was not the girl who walked confidently through the halls at school. I limped. I wore awkward, boxy shoes. The princesses in the tales I read at school and at home were not hampered by orthopedic inserts or physical therapy. They didn't have to go on yearly checkups to a hospital in Toronto so a doctor could examine their misshapen feet and measure their limbs.

Princesses did not get made fun of at school because *they walk so funny*. Princesses were not nicknamed *Pickle* because *you walk like there's a pickle stuck up your ass!* (Except that sometimes, to my much later surprise, they were – 'Cinderella' is a nickname given to our heroine by her stepmother and stepsisters, who bully and make fun of her for the ashes that settle on her hands and her hair due to her work as a scullery maid.)

The princesses I knew were graceful and beautiful and danced like a dream. I also knew objectively that they were not *real*, but how could I argue with the swell of my heart when Aurora's gown changed from blue to pink and back again? How to argue with the very obvious able-bodied beauty of Disney's Belle or Cinderella, or the inevitable way so many fairy-tale endings arc toward romance? How to square that away with my sense of self as someone who would never be beautiful in exactly that kind of way? More importantly – how to realize that being beautiful *in that kind of way* isn't actually the thing that matters? How to wrestle with the inevitability of life's divergence from the traditional happy-ending arc when those traditional happy endings were everywhere – in fairy tales, in the media, in other stories I read and loved? How to recognize that it isn't life's divergence from this arc that is the problem, but the establishment of this arc in the first place – these able-bodied ideals, these able-bodied expectations?

And how to wrestle with this difference between the able-bodied arc and the disabled one when disability is so entirely absent from these happy endings?

Cerebral. From the French *cérébral,* which comes from the Latin *cerebrum,* meaning the brain. In medical terms it refers to the area of the brain in and around the cortex, and the connections that run from there to the cerebellum.

Palsy. This time Anglo-French by way of Latin: paralysis, meaning 'loosening,' which became *paralasie,* which then became palsy, or 'disease causing paralysis.'

Together, an umbrella term for a number of conditions that restrict and order movement, or don't allow it at all.

Other uses of *cerebral*: of or relating to the brain. Involving intelligence rather than emotion or instinct.

Palsy (noun): complete or partial muscle paralysis, often accompanied by loss of sensation and uncontrollable body movements or tremors. A weakening or debilitating influence. A fit of strong emotion marked by the inability to act.

Verb: to paralyze, to deprive of strength.

To make helpless, as with fear.

In his 1986 consult notes to my family GP, Dr. Humphreys is calm and matter-of-fact, clinical, and also warm and generous. *The child was born of a full term normal pregnancy, uncomplicated delivery and weighed 8lbs 6oz. The child's subsequent development was reasonably unremarkable. However, at about the age of six months, it was noticed that Amanda's right toes 'did not relax and remained curled.' She was then slow to walk and was not taking steps securely until she was seventeen months of age by which time she was fairly independent with her gait. But even then, her balance was unsteady and her foot tended to turn in.*

He is definitely a storyteller.

As time passed, and she became more active, she would often walk by swinging her right leg into a circle. She has never run with any aggression. Her gait abnormally persists, and accordingly, a search has been made for possible impairments in her right forearm and hand. There is very little to detect there, even in terms of subtle arm posturing. However, for whatever reason, she has become left-handed.

(Once upon a time, left-handedness was thought to have come from the Devil. Matthew 25:41: *Then shall he say also unto them on the left hand, depart from me, ye cursed, into everlasting fire, prepared for the devil and his angels.* It was a mark of all things inferior and wrong: Eve, who developed from Adam's left rib and side; women in general, who were thought to descend from a man's left testicle during copulation, thus leading to the practice in Ancient Greece of men tying off one testicle in order to control the sex of their offspring. Zulu tribes in nineteenth-century South Africa would place a child's left hand in boiling water to burn it and force the child to use the right hand instead; during the Spanish Inquisition, the Catholic Church feared that the left-handed were witches and occasionally burned them alive.

Cesare Lombroso, considered by many to be the father of criminology, wrote in 1903 that 'as man advances in civilization and culture, he shows an always-greater righthandedness as compared to savages, the masculine in this way outnumbering the feminine and adults outnumbering children.' Lombroso saw left-handedness as a marker of abnormality – a *disability* that separated the haves and have-nots.

Dr. Humphreys, of course, did not believe that a child who was left-handed was also inferior. But are we surprised, after so many centuries of story and belief, to hear the incredulity in his voice, the speculation? *For whatever reason, she has become left-handed.*)

At present the motor disability is quite mild and appears to involve only her right leg and specifically, the ankle and foot. Her parents have noted that it is taking her a longer time to walk specified distances, such as to and from school and through a shopping centre. It has been noted along the way that she has a minor head tilt to the left which presumably relates to a squint, slight wasting of the right calf, and very mild caudal scoliosis.

On clinical examination, the child is quite alert and co-operative. However, she does have a very mild spastic hemiparetic gait, almost involving the right leg entirely. She develops an equinovarus foot on which she limps.

Hemiparetic: from *hemiparesis*, denoting weakness of one side of the body. From the ancient Greek *hemipleges*, 'stricken on one side.'

Equinovarus: an elevated foot ('equine,' like a horse's) that turns downward and in. *Ialipes equinovarus* – the most common term for *club foot*, that famous condition through which Oedipus was marked by the gods.

But then, is Oedipus always spoken of as a disabled man? His disability is more often than not spoken of *symbolically*, a marker of how his parents try to outwit the gods. It is an essential part of a narrative about a man who tries, again and again, to escape fate. His disability is not a fact of life – something that becomes mundane to him, something that merely exists alongside him and within him, *of* him, as he moves through the world. It is a symbol that pushes his story forward in a particular way – he must overcome it, move above it, prove himself worthy because, as a man with a foot unlike that of other men, singled out for punishment due to his parents' transgression, he is automatically seen as less.

Oedipus's club foot becomes the key through which his narrative reaches forward to completion: to overcome his disability, he must bow to the fact that the gods have ordained it, have visited it on him as a symbol of his *hubris* in trying to defy fate. To overcome the realities of trouble that the club foot introduces into his life, he – and we, as the readers of his tale – must instead see it as a symbol of something else, some other ill or wrong that, once righted, will allow him to triumph in the way that all other abled heroes do. And so the lived reality of this disability becomes something else, abstract and ephemeral, making it that much harder to see disability as a concrete reality in the world.

The first time I thought of Oedipus as a disabled man was only recently, in researching this book. That's what disability-as-symbol does in the stories that we tell.

Or, as Tobin Siebers puts it, 'No one ever sees Sophocles' play as a drama about a cripple and a blind man fighting over Thebes.'

'Reading disability merely as a metaphor for something else is in itself a form of erasure,' notes Ann Schmiesing, 'because it abstracts the individual and his or her disabled body.'

But my cerebral palsy has never been a *symbol* of anything. It has only ever been me – me, myself, my body. So how does the path go forward from here? The stories we tell, the symbols we use. In a society that so often uses the disabled body as a symbol of some inner ill, how do we move forward and reclaim the messy, lived complexity of what it means to have a different body in the world?

Disability: A Fairy Tale

Disabled:
1a: impaired or limited by a physical, mental, cognitive, or
developmental condition : affected by disability
b: incapacitated by illness or injury
2: of a device or mechanism : rendered inoperative (as by
being damaged or deliberately altered)

In English, the word *disabled* comes to us as the past participle of *disable*. From the Latin *dis* ('to do the opposite of') and the Old French *(h)able* ('capable, fitting, suitable, agile, nimble'), itself from the Latin verb *habere* – to hold and receive. It came into use as a term in the sixteenth century. Once used primarily for impairments of a physical nature, it is now widely recognized as a term that applies to all manner of impairments. According to the World Health Organization, *disabilities*

> is an umbrella term, covering impairments, activity limitations, and participation restrictions. An impairment is a problem in body function or structure; an activity limitation is a difficulty encountered by an individual in executing a task or action; while a participation restriction is a problem experienced by an individual in involvement in life situations. Disability is thus not just a health problem. It is a complex phenomenon, reflecting the interaction

between features of a person's body and features of the society in which he or she lives.

It is a complex phenomenon in part due to the growing prevalence of the *social model* of disability, which holds that the disability of individuals is, in fact, maintained by systemic barriers, exclusion, and negative attitudes toward these disabilities more than the physical limitations of the conditions themselves. (If a building has elevators and accessible entryways, the fact that a person uses a wheelchair doesn't limit them in the building in any way; by contrast, a building with an inaccessible doorway and no elevators is a barrier because a person with accessibility needs cannot go through it, thus indicating that, on a structural level, the design of the building has failed to take the considerations of every different body into account.) The social model of disability stands in contrast to the *medical model*, which links a body directly to a diagnosis and places emphasis on the intervention of medicine as a way of solving or eradicating the particular disability or condition. 'The medical model,' notes Tobin Siebers, 'defines disability as an individual defect lodged in the person, a defect that must be cured or eliminated if the person is to achieve full capacity as a human being.' It's not that society needs to be fixed, in other words – it's the person who is broken. 'Medicine and charity,' says Siebers, '[and] not social justice, are the answers to the problem of the disabled body, because the disabled body is thought to be the real cause of the problems.'

In the medical model, disability is both a reality of life as well as a kind of storytelling. Every disabled story becomes a narrative – a story that has everything to do with what culture perceives of as good (able-bodiedness, beauty) and bad (disability, disfigurement), and how we, as a society, are supposed to act toward one another – and what society, or the higher powers that be, will do to us in return. Quite apart from its own physical realities – from the disabled person's own physical realities – a disability thus becomes a symbol for everyone else, an 'other other,' in Siebers's words, operating as a kind of intellectual bogeyman for the well – a whispering darkness that sits on the edge of the perceived order of the world.

In short, in the medical model, disability is almost always the villain. Disability is *different* because there is an assumption that there is one way of moving through the world – one way of walking, one way of seeing, one way of smell and touch, of processing information. Deviations from this assumption must therefore both require and generate explanations. A child is born with a cyst in her brain but *should have* been born with none, and therefore the reasons for it must be uncovered: genetic defect, in-utero injury, identifiable condition. Otherwise, how to place her? How to understand where she fits into the world? The narrative around her disability follows the same structure as the fairy tales she reads in bed at night with her mother: problem, quest, return. In the medical model, the 'return' involves the acquisition/reacquisition of an able-bodied life inasmuch as this is possible – think gene therapy, think cochlear implants, think searching for a *cure*.

But before we had the medical model, before we had science, we had storytelling in all of its inscrutable magic. How else to make sense of a child born with a malformed limb than by telling a story about it – encasing the limb in a glass coffin of story that reaches back to magic and the gods, ever inscrutable themselves? Stories impose order even on unruly bodies. When you make something inconceivable into a story, suddenly it gains legitimacy, suddenly it operates in the realm of the possible.

So, too, with bodies that are different.

'Fairy tales,' argues the renowned fairy-tale scholar Jack Zipes, 'are informed by a human disposition to action – to transform the world and make it more adaptable to human needs, while we also try to change and make ourselves fit for the world. Therefore, the focus of fairy tales, whether oral, written, or cinematic, has always been on finding magical instruments, extraordinary technologies, or powerful people and animals that will enable protagonists to transform themselves along with their environment, making it more suitable for living in peace and contentment.'

Fairy tales are among those most quintessential of stories – the ones we tell to make sense of ourselves and of the world. They are both a way of explaining the world around us and a method of imagining a world that is possible. 'Early oral tales,' notes Zipes, 'were closely tied to the rituals, customs and beliefs of tribes, communities and trades. They fostered a sense of belonging and hope that miracles involving some kind of magical transformation were possible to bring about a better world.'

Imagining a world that is *possible* becomes particularly important when one considers fairy tales in light of the times in which they were told. It is hard to conceive of the possibility of a CT scan when you live in a society that hasn't yet discovered electricity; it is much easier to conceive of and believe in magic, and so too in potions and fairy dust and magical godmothers, or genies who can grant wishes. Fairy tales have in so many ways concerned themselves with transformation. But because their creators – perhaps particularly in the Western world –

were often not able to envision the full possibilities of science and technology, the transformations in the fairy tales that we know have necessarily been limited in crucial ways.

In 'Hans My Hedgehog,' a tale from the Brothers Grimm, a farmer, despairing of his and his wife's inability to have a child (a despair magnified by the other farmers mocking their childlessness), exclaims that he would be happy to have a child, 'even if it's a hedgehog.' Their son, Hans My Hedgehog, born nine months after this proclamation, is born with the upper half of a hedgehog and the bottom half of a human. Horrified, the parents keep their son behind the stove for seven years, ultimately forcing Hans to go out into the world on his own to make his fortune as a musician (he has his father bring him back a set of bagpipes from the market) and herder and tender of geese and pigs.

Hans is a plucky protagonist, unafraid, despite his parents' treatment of him, to ask for what he wants and demand betterments in life. He gradually amasses a reputation as an excellent herder, becoming so successful at it that he is able to return to his childhood home with a herd of pigs he sells to benefit the town.

Sale behind him, Hans My Hedgehog goes out into the world once again and meets a king who has lost his way. In exchange for directions, the king agrees to give Hans My Hedgehog his daughter in marriage; however, once the king has found his way and realizes the full extent of the bargain he has made – marrying his daughter off to a half-human creature – he is reluctant to carry it out. For her part, the daughter is less than pleased. As punishment for her distaste, Hans My Hedgehog has the princess take off her clothes, then stabs her with his quills until she's covered in blood. She flees from him in disgrace, never to return to her kingdom.

Sometime later, Hans My Hedgehog encounters another king who has gotten lost in the forest. This king is also accepting of Hans My Hedgehog's help, but, more importantly, is amenable to the price of it; as a result, Hans My Hedgehog returns to this king's castle and manages to get himself married to the princess. It is to her and her alone that he reveals his greatest secret: his hedgehogness is only a costume, a disguise he can take off at night. He instructs the princess and the king to have four guards grasp his hedgehog suit when he removes it and throw it onto the fire, thereby banishing his hedgehogness forever and assuming his true, permanent guise as an attractive young man. This feat accomplished, Hans My Hedgehog is able to return to his parents, beautiful princess wife in tow, and rejoice with them at the ultimate triumph over his disfigurement. His father, overjoyed at this appearance of a 'normal' son, is kind to Hans My Hedgehog for the rest of his life.

'Hans My Hedgehog' is interesting because it relies on both the protagonist's self-advocacy and a deep undercurrent of social expectation. Hans is vocal about his wants and needs, and presses his father to let him go out into the world and live an independent life. He proves himself as a character worthy of respect by becoming quite successful at herding the pigs. He is also a character of no small musical skill; the first king, hearing the beauty of his bagpipe music in the forest, remarks on the unseen player's talent. In his continued work to prove who he is to the world, Hans My Hedgehog is advocating for *social* change: he wants society to accept him as he is, to recognize the gifts he can bring to the community, hedgehog or no. There is a constant sense throughout the tale that Hans My Hedgehog is being unfairly treated by those he encounters. He is scorned by his parents, and the first king who meets him is reluctant to give away his daughter due to his distaste for Hans My Hedgehog's appearance. The daughter herself is also ashamed to be around him, and punished for her attitude. It is only the kind king and the willing princess who learn the truth about Hans – a reward, if you will, for their good behaviour.

And yet, toward the end of the tale, we have the standard fairy-tale transformation/reveal: the hedgehogness is only a suit, one that Hans My Hedgehog can take off at will. Hans My Hedgehog gets the homecoming that one senses the narrator has been rooting for all along: the reunification of his family and the quiet, relieved joy of the princess, who, kindness notwithstanding, likely much prefers her human husband to his previous half-animal form.

Whether it's the pumpkin in 'Cinderella' or the sudden appearance of the Little Mermaid's human legs, fairy tales often pivot on something or someone becoming different at some point through the text – the unattainable suddenly made manifest through magic, fairy dust, and longing. The evil fairy transforms a spinning wheel into an instrument of death in 'Sleeping Beauty'; the wolf transforms/disguises himself in 'Little Red Riding Hood.' Cinderella herself transforms from a scullery maid into a princess.

But it is never society that changes, no matter how many half-animals or scullery maids are out there arguing for their place at the table. It is almost always the protagonists themselves who transform in some way – becoming more palatable, more beautiful, more easily able to fit into the mould of society already in place. The intervention is magical rather than surgical, but one can imagine the writers of these tales arguing in favour of the medical model: the *life-saving* surgery, where *life* is synonymous with social standing and regard. The child who has surgery to repair their club foot is the same child who, in a fairy tale, would likely be visited by a fairy godmother or an evil witch, the gift of able-bodiedness dangled in front of them in a way that's entirely irresistible.

In fairy tales, the transformation of the individual relies on fairies and magic – or the gods – because it is understood that society itself can't (and indeed won't) improve. Again, when viewed in the historical context of the tales, this makes at least a small amount of sense; how to fix the world when you are a peasant with a disabled child, possessed of little to no power to change the place and society in which you live? And yet the power of magic in the tales also, strangely, has the opposite effect – instead of imbuing the reader with a worldview in which change is possible and things can turn out positively for the disenfranchised, the prevalence of magic in fairy tales serves to reinforce the class and societal structures already in place, as well as traditional ideas of what it means to have a functional body in the world. This is possibly why there's almost always a price that a protagonist pays for the magic of their transformation. You cannot simply move from one place to the next – society won't allow it. And so the protagonist must prove their worthiness – through good deeds and gentle behaviour, as in the case of Cinderella, or, as with the Little Mermaid, through sacrifice and trial.

Failing that, perhaps one can find a magic fairy, or, as in many of the Brothers Grimm tales, shore up their belief in God. 'While championing health and able-bodiedness as the ideal,' says Ann Schmiesing, 'tales in the [Brothers Grimm] frequently suggest that this ideal is unattainable, at least without divine intervention.'

To walk, to see, to hear, to touch. Gifts worth all their trouble, no matter what price must be paid.

I'm four years old, soon to be five, when I leave the hospital for the first time, after the surgery where they opened my head and sliced out bits of the cyst. I am excited to be going home. My mother and I have read all of the *Little House on the Prairie* books while here, some of them twice. (*On the Banks of Plum Creek* is my favourite. I like the idea of Mary and Laura Ingalls living in a dugout and running through the grass on their own roof.)

One day close to the end of my three-week stay, I come back to my hospital room with the nurse and find my mother and grandmother standing beside Dr. Humphreys.

'We have three dresses for you,' Dr. Humphreys says. He smiles. I like his smile a lot. 'But you can only wear one of them! So you need to pick which one you want to wear.'

This is a celebration dress − I know this even when I'm four. We are celebrating because soon I'm not going to be in the hospital anymore. Soon I won't have any bandages. Soon Margaret the nurse won't need to wash my head and help me bathe.

I don't remember what the other dresses looked like, but the dress I pick is pale green. It has short sleeves, and two lines of pink ribbon down the front. The skirt puffs out when I twirl, even though I can't twirl very fast because of the bandages.

I love it. It makes me feel like a princess.

In the social model of disability, the 'return' from the quest involves a recognition of the different body and how it fits, differently, into the world − and from there, a recognition of how society in turn must adapt to welcome it. '[D]isabling environments,' writes Siebers, 'produce disability in bodies and require interventions at the level of social justice.' The social model arose in the 1960s as a response, by disabled people, to the patriarchal nature of and infantilization inherent in the medical model. Transcripts from a 1975 meeting between the UK Disability Alliance and the Union of the Physically Impaired Against Segregation stress the point: 'In our view it is society which disables physically impaired people. Disability is something imposed on top of our impairments by the way we are unnecessarily isolated and excluded from full participation in society.' ('Physically impaired' is historical language; though it was in use at the time of the quote, *impaired* is generally considered to be language not acceptable to use in reference to the disability community today.) The social model of disability as a specific term was coined in the UK in 1983 by the disabled academic Mike Oliver.

In the social model, there is emphasis on creating space for wheelchairs that accommodate a body that cannot walk, as opposed to the need to walk at all costs; there is the growing recognition of the need for things like ASL interpretation and scent-free spaces at public events; there is, as I have touched on, the acknowledgement that public events and spaces that do not offer accessible entryways or accessible washrooms fail to consider the varied needs of the population. There is, above all, the push for disabled people to be involved in all aspects of decisions regarding their participation in society – and the recognition that society has a responsibility toward *all* of its citizens, up to and including the need to consider how best to meet the varying needs of different bodies. *Nothing about us, without us* – a saying that has been associated with the disability justice movement since the 1990s – encompasses much of the ethos that underpins the social model.

The social model of disability has steadily gained traction in the years since its inception. As with other justice movements in the early twenty-first century, the advent of social media has proven particularly helpful and galvanizing for disability justice activists, providing an accessible platform that many disabled individuals are able to access and participate in, economic barriers (access to the internet, to a computer, to a mobile phone, to libraries) notwithstanding. In the last few years alone, Twitter hashtags like #DisabledAndCute (started by Black disabled writer and activist Keah Brown), #Things-DisabledPeopleKnow (started by Black disabled writer and activist Imani Barbarin), and #DisabilityTooWhite (started by Black disabled activist and blogger Vilissa Thompson) have done much to push the conversation about disability, the social model, and access into mainstream public attention.

This is also a kind of storytelling, though firmly set in modern packaging. But though the medium of telling is relatively new, the act of storytelling itself has a long history of speaking truth to power. The trick here is to tell stories in a way that outlines injustice but also calls on the community and the social structures in place to change so that *anyone* – and not just a select few – might also be able to reach for success in the future.

'Telling stories – that is, command of the word – was vital if one wanted to become a leader, shaman, priest, priestess, king, queen, medicine man, healer, minister, and so on, in a particular family, clan, tribe, or small society,' writes Jack Zipes in *The Irresistible Fairy Tale*. He argues that fairy tales, by their very nature, speak to the longing for justice that bubbles deep in every human heart – the ability to tell a story that captivated was, in bygone times, an essential part of governance, inextricably bound up with power. It is arguably still an essential part of governance today – one need only look to the words of people like Barack Obama to acknowledge the ability that words and stories have to inflame the minds and hearts of a generation.

Conversely, one need also only look to the words of someone like Donald Trump to see how words can also do the opposite – pack prejudice and fear into tightly controlled narratives that then infect the thoughts of many. In these instances, stories become narratives that champion the individual's triumph as opposed to narratives that change the world so everyone can win. Perhaps more importantly, stories become narratives that champion the individual's triumph specifically *at the expense* of those who do not win – a process of othering that has wide-ranging implications.

In *Illness as Metaphor*, Susan Sontag notes that 'modern totalitarian movements have been peculiarly – and revealingly – inclined to use disease imagery.' Thus did we see Donald Trump tweet on June 19, 2018, that '[Democrats] want illegal immigrants, no matter how bad they may be, to pour into and *infest* our Country, like MS-13' (italics mine). Thus did David Ward, a former US immigration officer, talk on Fox News in October 2018 of migrants who bring diseases 'such as smallpox and leprosy and [tuberculosis] that are going to infect our people in the United States.' In this kind of real-world storytelling, the fear-mongering is focused specifically on the aspect of disease – and, by extension, disability – as something that *others*. To avoid it, we must also avoid the *people* who are suffering. Because nobody wants to be other, even by association. In this way, telling stories – command of the word – often works to disenfranchise those who are already disenfranchised, further decreasing their own chances of success and thereby increasing the continued success of a particular few.

Put another way: the medical model celebrates an individual's triumph over disability, while the social model celebrates society's collective power and responsibility to consider the needs of all, thus making disability an integrated element of the society in which we live.

(It should be noted that the social model is not without its criticism. In particular, recent critiques note that it is not always possible to improve the social environment so that all aspects of a disability are accounted for and mitigated. Ramps might help a wheelchair user into a store, but ramps and accessible washrooms do not erase pain or fatigue – and the push for social adjustments that account for certain aspects of a disability but not all can often have the effect of silencing those who might speak about their pain or other difficulties but do not, for fear of seeming to speak against the social model itself.)

Disabled people, along with other marginalized groups, have long borne the brunt of disenfranchisement in storytelling, which is why the explosion of social media offers such a powerful opportunity. In demanding the space to tell our own stories, in advocating for the social model of disability and for its different ways of viewing the world, disabled people are taking back control of the narrative, and urging the world to rethink the idea of the individual triumph, doing the work of dismantling the narratives that have been told about disabled people for thousands of years.

And yet these narratives run so much deeper than we realize. Like the thorns that grew to submerge Sleeping Beauty's castle in the Disney film, their roots run gnarled paths far below the ground. To understand how the medical and social models of disability function in the world of our everyday, and how these models and ways of thinking shape the words that guide countries on a social, political, and structural level, we must also understand how the stories that we've told in the past have worked to entrench the idea of the disabled *other* as – at best – an object of pity, and at worst an invisible someone, barely there at all.

In *Care Work*, author and disability activist Leah Lakshmi Piepzna-Samarasinha explores the rise of disability justice against the specific concerns and experiences of Black, POC, and queer disability politics. In looking specifically at disabled IBPOC survivor narratives, Piepzna-Samarasinha raises the spectre that haunts most of the fairy tales we know – this question of there being only two ways for a story to end. '[S]omething terrible and murky happens in a bedroom,' they write, 'there's a lot of DARKNESS, and then the sun comes out, you speak to a nice therapist in a pastel office for six sessions, and then you're fixed, you marry your husband or get a girlfriend and have a kid, and it's all pastel soft lighting fade out forever. You either do that or you're fucked – you abuse your kids, and you die a horrible death. Those are the two options in the back of folks' heads.'

These two options – happiness forever or terrible tragedy and sadness until death – sit in the backs of our heads in many ways because of the stories we've all been told as children. Happy endings are happy precisely *because* they have no darkness – unhappy endings, conversely, are that way because of a total absence of happiness and light.

For many able-bodied people in the world today, the idea of disability comes shrouded in darkness. It is inconceivable to so many that someone could be disabled and also happy, because we as social beings have been taught, through the books we read and the films and television we watch and the music we listen to, the stories we tell one another, that to be disabled is to be at a disadvantage: to be a lesser body, to be a body that cannot function at the same level as other bodies in society. To be disabled is to be in pain, physically and psychologically, emotionally and spiritually – and what possible goodness can be found in pain? What sort of happy ending can be found in constant struggle?

(And yet society also parrots an accompanying surface truth: that we are all individuals, that we all have different ways of being in the world. Of *course* life isn't all happy endings, society says – while simultaneously venerating happiness and joy and shying away from struggle and pain. Of *course* the larger world believes – in an intellectual, thought-exercise kind of way – that it is possible to be happy and also disabled – until that same larger world is faced with the specific complexities of what it means to occupy the disabled body. Of *course* society can expand and grow and change to account for bodies of all types   until that body is seen as unreasonable, or demanding, or wanting 'special treatment,' in which case the world falls back on the ableism that has underpinned our stories for centuries, and lets out a resounding cry of *that's unfair*.

It's unfair that disabled people get special treatment. It's unfair that disabled people get to park closer, or that disabled people get discounts, or that disabled people are allowed to bring their service animals into a restaurant. It's unfair that disabled people get to stay at home while other people have to go out and work!)

Often, the medical and social models of disability embody this happy/unhappy dichotomy – and depending on where you're standing, the question of which model represents the happy ending is open to interpretation. Proponents of the medical model see the disabled life as an unhappy ending because the medical model can fix it; proponents of the social model see the prospect of a cure as an unhappy ending because it removes the responsibility of bettering the social environment from society at large and places the onus on the individual to transform, thus eradicating the physical differences and accompanying memories that so often tether the disabled person's experience of the world.

Who would I be, for example, if I hadn't been born the girl with the cyst in her brain? My experiences at the hospital and with surgeries, with the wheelchair and my crutches, with my limp and the eventual bullying that came about as a result of all of this – these experiences have shaped me, have made me who I am. Had I been born without that cyst, I would have a different life now. I would not be who I am today.

In *Disability Theory*, Siebers advances a theory of what he terms *complex embodiment*, wherein elements of both the medical model and the social model guide how the body makes its way through the world. 'The theory of complex embodiment,' he writes, 'raises awareness of the effects of disabling environments on people's lived experience of the body, but it emphasizes as well that some factors affecting disability, such as chronic pain, secondary health effects, and aging, derive from the body.'

In effect, it is possible to be disabled both by society and by pain; to struggle both as a result of the overwhelming bias in favour of the able body and as a result of the unique nature of one's own body and its different challenges in the world. Disability and able-bodiedness are both merely points on an enormous spectrum of human variation, and the work of being in the world at all entails being on this spectrum in some way, shape, or form.

It is not hard to travel from this reality of a spectrum of disability through to a subsequent spectrum of happiness, where it is possible to recognize *happiness*, like ability and disability, as a malleable, changeable quality that doesn't exist in static form. Just as it is possible to move from ability to disability – and also possible, through innovations both medical and social, to move from disability to ability and back again – so too is it possible (and, in fact, more realistic) to move from happiness to unhappiness and back again, over and over, as we move through life.

We mustn't tell this to the princess, however. Who is she if she can't walk down the aisle to meet her prince?

In the Brothers Grimm's 'The Maiden Without Hands,' a miller is visited by the Devil, disguised as an old man, who promises the miller riches in exchange for whatever lies beyond his mill. The miller, thinking the Devil means an old apple tree, gladly makes the bargain; it is only when he returns home to his wife, who is overjoyed at the jewels and money that now overflow their cupboards, that he discovers the truth: his daughter, beautiful and pious, was standing on the other side of the mill when the Devil struck his bargain.

In three years, the Devil returns to claim the maiden. First she draws a circle round herself and purifies it with water so he can't get to her; then, when the Devil angrily instructs the father to rid the house of water so she can't purify herself anymore, she weeps onto her hands and purifies them with her tears.

'Chop off her hands!' the Devil instructs, and the father, terrified, does as he is told.

But the maiden weeps over her stumps, purifying them once again, and the Devil retreats in defeat. The father, now a rich man, promises to look after his daughter for the rest of her life, but she refuses to stay. Instead, she instructs her father to tie her severed hands to her back and casts herself out onto the mercy of the world.

She comes to a kingdom, and a royal garden. Suffering from hunger, she falls to her knees and cries aloud to God; an angel appears and lets her into the garden, then brings her fruit from the trees. But she is discovered, and the angel vanishes. Thinking she's a thief, the soldiers throw her in the dungeon.

She is rescued by the king, who falls in love with her and brings her out of the dungeon. When they marry, the king gives her a pair of silver hands that she learns to use in place of her real ones. But the Devil, still angry at his thwarted attempt to take her, isn't finished. A year after their marriage, the king goes away to war and the Maiden Without Hands, now queen, gives birth to a son; the Devil intercepts the messenger who is bringing this news to the king and gives him a message to say that the queen has given birth to a changeling. The king reads the fake message and is distressed, but still loves his wife – he instructs the messenger to go back and tell the kingdom that his wife and the child must be protected.

But the Devil intercepts the message again, and the messenger brings back a falsified edict, purportedly from the king, that the queen and the child are to be killed. The king's old mother helps them both escape from the castle, and the Maiden Without Hands finds herself wandering the world again, this time with her child.

They come to a hut in the forest; an angel appears to them and tells the queen that she may stay there, untroubled. They live here for fourteen years until the king – who spent the first seven years fighting on the battlefield and then, having learned of the Devil's treachery, the last seven years searching the wilderness for his family – finally finds them again. They return to the kingdom and live happily for the rest of their days.

The queen's hands have grown back in the interim, as hands in fairy tales are wont to do if you pray hard enough.

Changeling, in itself, is an interesting term. Historically, the idea of a changeling child has been inextricably tied up with magic; in Irish folklore, changelings were thought to be the children of fairies who'd been swapped in for healthy human children. Fairy children were considered to be sickly, and it was often expected that they wouldn't live long; families would leave their 'changeling' children out to die in the cold as a result, convinced that their actual child was lost to them forever.

The belief was held that fairies swapped out human children for any number of reasons: for companionship, out of revenge, to have a human child as a servant. Usually, the suspicion that a child was a changeling arose right at birth; but in some cases, the question didn't come up until years later. In 1826 an Irish woman drowned a three-year-old boy in her care in the River Flesk because he couldn't speak or walk and she was trying to get 'the changeling out of him'; in 1895 the Irishwoman Bridget Cleary was killed by her husband and relatives after a short illness, with the husband invoking what became infamous as the 'fairy defence.'

Tellingly, the question of whether a child was a changeling or not was directly tied to whether the child showcased visible disabilities at birth – or, in cases of later development, whether the child/young person exhibited behaviour that was thought at the time to be incomprehensible or strange. Nineteenth-century beliefs posited that autistic children were the product of fairies – the belief that fairies themselves spent long amounts of time completing repetitive tasks like counting gold coins echoes documented elements of autistic behaviour. (If there is no worldly explanation, there is most assuredly a magical one.)

Consider them, for a moment. A child born with a caul, a boy with a club foot, a girl with spina bifida, left outside to shiver and cry until they are no more. A child three centuries ago, born with cerebral palsy, though no one yet knows what it is, only that the child can't eat or speak or roll over. Grief-stricken parents who curse the fairies and leave the child outside to die of starvation or exposure. Children who aren't magical, but only different.

How many children have we lost to the cold and snow over the centuries – children born not to a king and queen but to common people, mothers and fathers with no knowledge of the world apart from the stories they've told themselves at night before their fires? How many lives have been smothered or disappeared or haven't been allowed to flourish because of the stories we tell?

'The Maiden Without Hands,' notes Ann Schmiesing, stands in stark opposition to a tale like 'Hans My Hedgehog,' precisely because the maiden is meek and subservient, where Hans My Hedgehog is a vocal activist in his own life. The maiden is ready and willing to cast herself into the world, to believe that society will meet all of her needs, whereas Hans My Hedgehog is instead focused on proving himself within the confines of the system. In contrast to Hans My Hedgehog's rage and advocacy, the Maiden's faith is as much an undercurrent throughout the tale as is her amputation.

It's tempting to think that 'The Maiden Without Hands' espouses the social model of disability, wherein disabled individuals operate within the world as a result of a society that takes care of their needs. But, in reality, this fairy tale operates squarely within the realm of the disabled charity trope, which many if not all modern disabled people recognize in some form or another.

The *charity model* shares similarities with the medical model of disability in that the disabled person is once again seen as a flaw – as someone in possession of a less-than-perfect body, a disfigured body, someone who is set apart from society as a result of these differences. In each case, the disabled person is at the mercy of others – in the medical model, medical professionals are the experts who can help the disabled individual and ultimately, hopefully, eradicate the disability; in the charity model, the disabled person is someone to be pitied and saved by both the medical and social establishments. The medical world will work to cure the physical, while the social world will work to improve the life of the disabled person through charity and magnanimous good deeds.

The charity model, as noted by the online resource *Disabled World*, '[d]epicts disabled people as victims of circumstance who are deserving of pity.' It relies on the time-honoured tradition of *noblesse oblige* (where those with means – literally, the 'nobles' – are obligated to improve society by giving back and sharing their wealth), but instead of the rich giving to the poor, the able-bodied are posited as those who instead deign to help the disabled. Yet while the idea of being charitable certainly seems like a nice thing to aspire to – the philanthropist is inevitably seen as a more morally acceptable figure than Ebenezer Scrooge – it's worth noting that charity also functions as a way of reinforcing existing social structures. As long as individual people are *charitable*, as long as individual charities and charitable actions exist to make gestures toward those who are less fortunate, there is less need for the sweeping societal change that would do away with the hierarchies and gross economic and structural inequalities that disadvantage people in the first place. Essentially, the existence of charity, by making concern for one's fellow humans less a *responsibility* and more an active choice, works to undermine the eradication of poverty and injustice.

(I am not, of course, arguing against the presence of charities – I think charities can and do accomplish wonderful things. It's good to encourage people to think of ways they can give to the world, and especially to think of how they might consider *those less fortunate*; the key is that we need to stop thinking of those less fortunate as being so because of some specific circumstance [disability, say] and more because of structural inequalities that the 'more fortunate' continue to uphold no matter how much money they give away.)

In *Illness as Metaphor*, Susan Sontag notes that disease has often been associated with moral failings.

> Psychological theories of illness are a powerful means of placing the blame on the ill. Patients who are instructed that they have, unwittingly, caused their disease are also being made to feel that they have deserved it … Nothing is more punitive than to give a disease a meaning – that meaning invariably being a moralistic one.

In literature, this has also been the case with disability. In the same way that sufferers of a disease become poster children for the ravages of the disease itself (TB, cancer, AIDS), disabled people become iterations of loss, of struggle, of the ways in which the world is not kind to those who are different. And in the same way that disease, for Sontag, then becomes a metaphor – something is a *cancer*, something spreads *like the plague* – so too does disability often become emblematic of these time-worn but still somehow newly urgent fears: loss of independence, social ostracization, loneliness in an increasingly connected world.

And in the same way that the medical model places the fault of disability at the body of the disabled person and lifts the medical professional up as the 'expert,' in the same way that the charity model removes the blame for society from the shoulders of the magnanimous philanthropist and reinforces hierarchical norms, psychological theories of illness lift the blame and responsibility for illness from the shoulders of society and place it squarely within the fault of the patient. If one had only refrained from some behaviour or practised others or been more devout or had more faith, the illness might have been avoided. (In the nineteenth and early- to mid-twentieth centuries, it was believed in some circles that melancholy patients might have avoided cancer if they had been happier; in the eighteenth century, those who were delicate and high-strung and prone to fits of excitability and high emotion might have avoided tuberculosis by practising a calmer, quieter kind of life.)

This sort of thinking sounds ridiculous now – except that when it comes to disability, it's often still engaged in, albeit in subtler (and arguably more damaging) ways. Disabled people are still brought to faith healers; they are told to drink more water or drink green tea or do detoxes or *try hypnosis to remove barriers of the mind* as a way of overcoming physical impairments. Disabled people are encouraged to 'push through' and 'exercise' and are reminded over and over again that *the only disability is a bad attitude*.

And when disabled people do manage to 'push through' in whatever way the able-bodied society sees fit, they are lauded as examples for all, as people who have refused to let themselves be 'confined' by their physical limitations in much the same way as people are spoken of as being 'confined' to a wheelchair.

Look at what you've overcome, society says. *You're such an inspiration*.

Inspiration porn, a phrase coined by the late Australian disability activist Stella Young in 2012, refers to the portrayal of disabled people as inspirational precisely because of their disability. Inspiration porn goes hand in hand with the idea of the disabled body as *less*. If a disabled body is seen as less, then what that body can achieve is also less – and yet somehow, paradoxically, more: more difficult, more noble, more *special*.

In an April 2019 article for *Bustle*, Imani Barbarin recounts going to a ballet class when she was seven. 'I wanted to develop art,' she wrote, 'but the teachers just wanted me to be seen. I wanted to be challenged, but no one challenges those born with "challenges."' Thus does the *less* of the disabled body become *more* in the eyes of the able-bodied world. The disabled body cannot meet the same bar as the body that is not disabled, and so the bar is lowered. When the disabled person meets the expectations of this new, lowered bar, they are cheered and congratulated.

You want to dance, but you have cerebral palsy and you'll never be a prima ballerina. So instead of creating a dance that responds specifically to the needs of your own body, you're given token representation and told you should be happy with being able to do this much.

Look at you, meeting this much lower bar. Look at you, trying to be like able-bodied people. That's more than enough – that's inspiring.

As with the charity model, psychological approaches to disability work to take the blame away from society and put it on the individual – to make disability not a lived, mundane reality but a temporary struggle that can be overcome if one has the inner and outer strength to do it. (The corollary here is that those who do not 'overcome' their disabilities – or fail to appreciate the so-called 'accomplishments' they make in the world of the disabled body's lowered bar – fail because of their own lack of strength or effort.)

Your disability is causing you pain? Do yoga. Struggling because of mental health issues? Meditate. The more you focus, the more you'll improve, and the less society at large needs to worry about having different kinds of dance classes or accessible entryways or accessible bathrooms or clearly marked accessible parking, to say nothing of captions or ASL or quiet rooms that offer respite from external stimuli.

After all, the *kingdom* didn't need to change for the Maiden Without Hands, did it? She got her hands back because of her faith. (*The only disability is a bad attitude.*)

She did that all on her own.

I'm six years old when I go back to school after both my surgeries. Grade 1. There is, as mentioned, a wheelchair, and a taxi that drives me to school. There is one half of a hexagonal table that I get to sit at all by myself because my wheelchair doesn't fit under the regular desks. There are classmates, again as mentioned, who are happy to push me around in the school-yard until they get bored and don't want to push me anymore. Sometimes – most times – it is easier to stay inside and read books, so that's what I do.

The cast on my leg begins to smell after a while; bathing is an ordeal because I am not allowed to get it wet. My mother has to help me because my right leg has to hang out of the tub at all times.

After the cast comes off, I work with a physiotherapist named Eric. He has dark hair and a beard and glasses and he reminds me of Robert Munsch (author of the beloved Canadian children's book *The Paper Bag Princess*). Or does Robert Munsch remind me of Eric the physiotherapist? I don't remember.

I don't remember much about this time, to be honest. The surgery, the two or three years after.

The memories start a bit later, when my nemesis arrives in Grade 3.

Cerebral palsy, traditionally, falls into four different classifications. The first classification, spastic cerebral palsy, refers to instances where muscle tightness and tone, or lack thereof, is the defining characteristic of the condition. The second type, ataxic cerebral palsy, is characterized by increased difficulty with fine motor skills, and difficulty with auditory and visual processing. The third type, dyskinetic or athetoid CP, is characterized by mixed muscle tone with involuntary motions. The fourth type, mixed CP, combines features of all four categorizations into one condition.

Symptoms can range from so minor as to be almost unnoticeable through to complete muscle paralysis. In 70 per cent of cases, CP is congenital – it arises out of some trauma or occurrence before birth. In my case, the cyst that caused the condition grew in my mother's womb alongside my neurons, my skull, my fingers and toes. Up until the end of high school, I had a MedicAlert bracelet that spelled it out for paramedics in the event of a disaster. *Spastic cerebral palsy, mild. VP shunt, disconnected.*

CP can also occur after birth. A traumatic entry via the birth canal, or the deprivation of oxygen soon after entry into the world. An umbilical cord looped tightly around the neck. Twenty per cent of cases happen this way. In the final 10 per cent of instances, the condition arises as a result of bacterial meningitis, viral encephalitis, and accidents or injuries that might occur from birth up to the age of three.

It is not a progressive condition, insofar as the initial brain injury that causes muscle difficulty doesn't worsen over time. There is no cure. Instead there are surgeries and physiotherapists, braces, special shoes.

Cysts like the one that grew in my head are a result of brain lesions, which themselves form after some kind of in-utero injury. The space left behind by a brain lesion fills with water and becomes a cyst. The cyst puts pressure on the brain, thereby damaging motor neurons, thereby impairing movement. A child walks with her foot turned inward. When that's fixed, a child limps.

But that child, that lucky child, gets to walk, after all. She can run. She can even dance, albeit not very well.

Why does it matter, then, if secretly that little girl wishes she could look like a princess; if she keeps pulling herself back to that moment in that green dress, leaving the hospital? What does this have to do with anything?

3

In Olden Times, When Wishing Still Helped:
The Fairy Tale in France and Germany

The explosion of the fairy tale in Europe in the sixteenth and seventeenth centuries began in Italy, with the collections of writers including Giovan Francesco Straparola (*The Pleasant Nights*, sometimes translated as *The Facetious Nights*) and Giambattista Basile (*The Pentamerone*).

Straparola, about whom not much is known, published *The Pleasant Nights* when he was living in Venice in 1550. In her book *Fairy Godfather: Straparola, Venice, and the Fairy Tale Tradition*, scholar and folklorist Ruth Bottigheimer notes that the name Straparola likely derives from the Italian verb *straparlare*, which means 'to talk too much' or to 'talk nonsense.' In the sixteenth and seventeenth centuries, it was not uncommon for fairy tales to be published under pseudonyms due to the satirical nature of some of the tales. Indeed, one of the tales first published in *The Pleasant Nights*, 'The Tailor's Apprentice,' was removed several years after first publication due to the influence of the Church, and the entire collection was placed on various lists of prohibited books from 1580 to 1624.

In a dedication at the beginning of the second volume of *The Pleasant Nights*, Straparola takes pains to note that the tales in the collection were not his original creations. It has also been put forth that some of the tales were actually taken from an earlier work by Italian lawyer Girolamo Morlini, who published a collection called *Novellae, fabulae, comoedia* in 1520. In any case, it is generally accepted that *The Pleasant Nights*, along with Basile's *Pentamerone*, stand as examples of collected, rather than original, fairy-tale creations.

Giambattista Basile was a poet and courtier as well as a collector of fairy tales. He was born, depending on which source you consult, in either 1566 or 1575 and spent a great deal of time serving as a soldier and courtier in Naples; *The Pentamerone*, for which he is best known, contains many fairy tales set in and around the Neapolitan kingdom. After he died in 1632, Basile's sister, Adriana, published *The Pentamerone* in two volumes in 1634 and 1636.

The Pentamerone contains some of the earliest known versions of several well-known Western fairy tales, including 'The Young Slave' (a variant of 'Snow White'), 'Pippo' (a variant of 'Puss in Boots'), and 'Sun, Moon, and Talia' (a variant of 'Sleeping Beauty'). Like Straparola's tales, the stories in these volumes were collected from the oral tradition, but instead of transcribing directly, Basile wrote the tales in the Neopolitan dialect, making heavy use of metaphor as fit the Baroque style of the time. Centuries later, the Brothers Grimm would praise *The Pentamerone* as the first 'national' collection of fairy tales.

In *When Dreams Came True: Classic Fairy Tales and Their Tradition*, Jack Zipes argues that as a port country playing host to a wide variety of merchants and businesspeople passing through on their way from the East to the rest of Europe and vice versa, Italy was an ideal breeding ground for the oral folk tale – and, as the world slowly began to disseminate more printed literature, an ideal place for these stories to be collected and spread throughout the populace.

Nonetheless, the stories of both Straparola and Basile remained outliers for a time. For much of the seventeenth century, many in France – where the next wave of interest in the folk tale would come – considered the folk tale beneath them, as it was by and large still being passed around in oral form at that time, often by the illiterate peasant class. But the advent of the *Bibliothèque bleue* – a series of small, light-blue chapbooks that began to be printed in France in the early 1600s and grew in circulation throughout the century, on subjects as wide-ranging as the theatre, etiquette, cookery, astrology, medieval verse, and folk tales – began to endear the fairy tale to a new, increasingly educated audience. In particular, French women of the aristocracy – who were not allowed to pursue higher education at the universities – began to organize literary salons where the tales were told and retold, polished and perfected into 'literary' form.

The major shift in the fairy tale's popularity in France came in the 1690s, in response to the Quarrel of the Ancients and Moderns, a debate among the aristocracy that pitted the ancient Greeks and Romans against modern French writers. Nicolas Boileau – a royal historiographer whose didactic work *L'Art poetique*, published in 1674, set out the rules of poetry composition in the classical tradition and partially ignited the debate – published an anti-feminist satire, 'Against Women,' in 1694, in response to the growing preference for modern French writers as arbiters of literary style. Boileau was part of a group who championed the ancient Greeks and Romans as models of art and literature for French society to follow. One of the main opponents to this thinking was Charles Perrault, the French author and member of the Académie française.

'Perrault,' notes Zipes, 'took the side of modernism and believed that France and Christianity … could only progress if they incorporated pagan beliefs and folklore and developed a culture of Enlightenment.'

Not surprisingly, many of the women who were telling literary fairy tales in the French salons of this time were also supporters of the modernists, a fact that is underlined by the subversive nature of the tales passed around by Perrault, Marie-Catherine Le Jumel de Barneville (the Baroness d'Aulnoy), and other writers of the time. '[Many] tales,' Zipes writes, 'displayed a certain resistance toward male rational precepts and patriarchal realms by conceiving pagan worlds in which the final "say" was determined by female fairies … [I]t is clear that the gifted French women writers at the end of the seventeenth century preferred to address themselves to a fairy and to have a fairy resolve the conflicts in their fairy tales, rather than the Church with its male-dominated hierarchy.' Indeed, the literary fairy tale became a powerful tool for the women of the court, who replaced traditional patriarchal figures of power not only with magical fairies, but with all-knowing wise women who acted as guiding forces for the protagonists. As well, many of their tales focused on love, again as a method of subversion – this time, speaking out against the prevalence of arranged marriage within the aristocracy itself.

The rise of the French literary salon was also a response to the increasingly stringent rule of Louis xiv; by the 1690s the king had created a system of absolute monarchial rule in France, angering many among the French nobility and aristocracy. The shape-shifting, seemingly innocuous nature of fairy tales became a subversive way to speak out against the administration. As Zipes points out, 'the French writers of fairy tales ... continued the "modernization" of an oral genre by institutionalizing it in literary form with utopian visions that emanated from their desire for better social conditions than they were experiencing in France at that time.'

Here we once again encounter the element of the fairy tale as utopian vision – a vision that, in reaching for a better world, sought to subvert expectation and press against structures of power in subtle yet crucial ways. Far from banal and innocuous – *it's only a story, after all* – fairy tales have often operated as coded messages, simultaneously spreading encouragement and hope to the disenfranchised and delivering scathing indictment of authorial figures, all within seemingly innocent trappings. The fairy godmother, for instance, spoke to the fact that Perrault thought a patron was necessary for an individual to triumph in the arts, offering a subtle yet damning pronouncement on the realities of making it as an artist in an increasingly capitalist world.

This is a tradition that has continued into modern times – writers like Angela Carter (whose story 'The Bloody Chamber' we will look at in Chapter Eight) and Kelly Link (author of the short story collections *Magic for Beginners* and *Get in Trouble*, among others) have explored the subversive nature of fairy tales in their own work, while many of the fairy-tale motifs that we know and love – the rags-to-riches princess (or prince), the animal helper, the fairy godmother – continue in popularity precisely because they can be subverted and used as allegories for larger social concerns. Princess Elizabeth, the titular heroine of *The Paper Bag Princess*, by Robert Munsch, subverts the standard damsel-in-distress trope after a dragon burns down her castle and kidnaps Prince Ronald, her fiancé. Instead of waiting for someone to come along and save them, Princess Elizabeth tracks down the dragon – clothing herself in a paper bag, as it's all that's left for her to wear out of her castle's ruins – and then challenges the dragon to burn forests down and fly around the world. When the dragon, having completed its second round-the-world trip, falls into an exhausted sleep, Princess Elizabeth rescues Ronald and saves the day.

But Ronald is ungrateful. Repulsed by her paper-bag trousseau, he tells her to go away and come back when she looks more like a princess. Instead of capitulating, Princess Elizabeth calls Ronald out – 'You look like a real prince, but you are a bum' – and the two do not, in fact, get married – a rallying cry for feminists everywhere.

Of note, however, is the conspicuous absence in these tales of subversion when it comes to disability. These stories might purport to reach for a better world, but the disabled body is only ever viewed by them as broken, and often only as worthy of a happy ending once the disability has been eradicated or otherwise 'overcome.' What does it say when some of the most subversive narratives we know continue to entrench and perpetuate static ideas about the disabled body?

In 1985, when I'm three years old, I dress up as a bride for Halloween. I have a white dress and a white veil and a tiny bouquet of pinkish-purple silk flowers. My sister is one and a half. She is dressed up as a superhero – a generic version, pre-Marvel Universe, with a red cape and a blue leotard and a dumbbell fashioned from cardboard that my mother covers over in foil – but doesn't really understand what's going on.

When my dad takes a video of the both of us, I smile straight into the heart of the camera.

'What are you, Amanda?'

'I'm a bride, Dad,' I say. You can tell that I know I am beautiful – that I love my white dress, the way that it twirls. I don't understand yet what being a bride really *means*, but I love the way that it feels. I seem special when I'm wearing the dress in a way that I don't when I have my regular clothes on. Like the dress that I'll wear out of the hospital in the not-so-distant future, I never want to take it off.

It is a gateway to something, though I don't yet know what that is. It whispers of possibility and happiness.

Years later, when I'm in university, I'll watch the 1989 Disney version of *The Little Mermaid* for the first time in years and think about how the last image I have of Ariel is of her on the wedding ship, joyously kissing her prince. About the way her story moves to a white dress as sign of completion. This is her happily ever after, this is the moment when she freezes in time.

She has more movement as a mermaid, as the body that is different from other bodies I know. This is the body that gets splashed across the movie promos, the body that sits on the cover of the DVD. The body without legs, the body that doesn't look like the bodies of everyone else.

I do not spend hours pretending to be Ariel in her wedding dress when I'm a child. I pretend that I'm a mermaid. I splash around in the pool and pretend that I don't have legs at all.

There is disfigurement and disability a-plenty in these old fairy tales from France, forgotten though so many of them may be. Specifically, there is a fascination with disfigurement and death as *punishment* – and, conversely, with the bestowing of beauty as the ultimate reward.

In 'Riquet with the Tuft,' an embedded tale within Catherine Bernard's 1696 novel *Inés de Cordoue*, the main character is a noblewoman, Mama, who is endowed with the outward traits of beauty but is intellectually disabled to such an extent that it 'make[s] her appearance distasteful.' The princess meets Riquet with the Tuft, an ugly little man who is king of the gnomes, and he makes her a bargain: if she agrees to marry him in a year's time, she will become intelligent. He gives her a verse and tells her to repeat it as often as possible, for it will teach her 'how to think.' Mama returns to her father's house, where she swiftly moves from 'coherent' to 'intelligent' to 'witty,' winning the hearts of all the men she encounters. But she loves only one: a man named Arada.

After the year has passed, Riquet with the Tuft returns for her hand in marriage. Mama is distressed, but Riquet gives her an ultimatum: remain intelligent and marry him as king of the gnomes, or return to her kingdom as the intellectually disabled woman she once was.

Mama chooses intelligence and marriage to the gnome – and she is now clever enough to conceive of ways to continue meeting Arada while still being married to Riquet. When her husband finds this out, he transforms himself to take on the likeness and manners of Arada, so that Mama is doomed to live the rest of her life with the two men, not knowing which of the two is her husband and which is the deceiver.

In Charles Perrault's version of 'Riquet with the Tuft,' published only a year after Bernard's novel, the intellectually disabled girl is a princess, and meets Riquet with the Tuft in the forest. Riquet himself is a prince, though ugly and misshapen, and has been given a gift by the fairies: he can endow his level of intelligence on the woman with whom he falls in love. Riquet is enchanted by the princess's beautiful portrait, which has circulated throughout the land, and has left his own kingdom to go in quest of her hand in marriage. In exchange for her hand – again in a year's time – he promises the princess a peculiar gift: "'I am able, madam," said Riquet with the Tuft, "to bestow as much good sense as it is possible to possess on the person whom I love the most. You are that person, and it therefore rests with you to decide whether you will acquire so much intelligence. The only condition is that you shall consent to marry me."'

Longing to move on the intellectual level of her peers, the princess agrees. Almost immediately, she becomes ferociously intelligent. She returns joyously to her kingdom and wows the court; she garners friends; her father the king comes to her for political and nation-building advice.

She also falls in love with a man, tall and handsome, and in a year, when the time has come to marry Riquet with the Tuft, she is overwhelmingly reluctant. Marry Riquet, the misshapen dwarf, when she has been pursued by a handsome man at court?

'With the exception of my ugliness,' says the dwarf, 'is there anything about me which displeases you? Are you dissatisfied with my breeding, my brains, my disposition, or my manners?' 'In no way,' replies the princess. 'I like exceedingly all that you have displayed of the qualities you mention.'

But Riquet has another gift. 'Let me tell you,' he says, 'that the same fairy who on the day of my birth bestowed upon me the power of endowing with intelligence the woman of my choice, gave to you also the power of endowing with beauty the man whom you should love, and on whom you should wish to confer this favor.'

The princess agrees to this, too, and Riquet is transformed into the handsomest man the princess has ever seen. This is followed by speculation from the narrator that Riquet, in fact, hasn't changed – only that the princess has been overcome with love for him and manages to 'see past' the qualities that she previously found so abhorrent:

Some people assert that this was not the work of fairy enchantment, but that love alone brought about the transformation. They say that the princess, as she mused upon her lover's constancy, upon his good sense, and his many admirable qualities of heart and head, grew blind to the deformity of his body and the ugliness of his face; that his humpback seemed no more than was natural in a man who could make the courtliest of bows, and that the dreadful limp which had formerly distressed her now betokened nothing more than a certain diffidence and charming deference of manner. They say further that she found his eyes shine all the brighter for their squint, and that this defect in them was to her but a sign of passionate love; while his great red nose she found naught but martial and heroic.

It's not surprising that the Perrault version of this tale is the one that has survived in ways that Catherine Bernard's version – and the tales of other French fairy-tale writers – have not. It is palatable in a way that the other version is not – softer and kinder, more given to beauty. There is a happy ending in this tale that is reminiscent of the bright Disney versions of fairy tales we've all come to know in the twentieth and twenty-first centuries. More importantly, however, in the overt moralizing of his tale, and the shaping of disability and deformity in particular as a kind of moral narrative that moves toward ability, Perrault's tale of 'Riquet with the Tuft' led the way to the stories that would go on to become the world's most famous: the collected fairy tales of the Brothers Grimm.

Jacob and Wilhelm Grimm were born in the town of Hanau, Germany, in 1785 and 1786, respectively. Three of their nine siblings died in infancy. In 1791 the Grimms moved to the town of Steinau, where their father, Philipp, worked as a magistrate. The family enjoyed relative wealth and prosperity until 1796, when Philipp died of pneumonia – a death that forced Jacob and Wilhelm, as the eldest sons, into positions of caring for their family's financial well-being while still only children themselves.

The brothers left home in 1798 for school, attending the Friedrichsgymnasium in Kassel. They graduated in 1803 and 1804, each with top honours, and went on to study at the University of Marburg, where their low social and economic standing made them acutely aware of their status as outcasts – a theme that would arise repeatedly in the tales they went on to collect and publish.

Originally intending to follow in their father's footsteps and practise law, Jacob and Wilhelm were sent on a meandering path toward folklore by dint of one of their law professors, Friedrich Karl von Savigny, who introduced them to the ideas of Johann Gottfried Herder, a German philosopher and literary critic who had, during his lifetime, championed *Naturpoesie*, or 'natural poetry,' as a superior and uniquely German method of storytelling.

According to Herder, *Naturpoesie* stood in opposition to *Artspoesie*, or 'artistic poetry,' because it preserved the robust nature of the German peasant life and with it those things that were thought to correlate to health and wellness – the fresh nature of the countryside as opposed to the damp, dank nature of cities and the havoc industrialization was wreaking upon landscapes moral, social, and economic. (The literary fairy tale, having begun its circles around the French court during Herder's lifetime, was seen – with all of its airs and literary figures of speech – to be encroaching on this nationalistic, 'true-to-nature' mode of storytelling.)

Jacob Grimm accepted a post as court librarian to the King of Westphalia in 1808, and Wilhelm followed some time later, after a visit to the region of Halle – financed by his brother – where he consulted with a physician about his ill health.

Wilhelm Grimm, of note, had been a strong and healthy child but grew ill with scarlet fever and asthma when he was sixteen; he was home from school for half the year and, though he recovered, illness returned in 1808; increasing in severity until he travelled to Halle in 1809 to seek treatment. His health remained precarious for the rest of his life, though he lived until the relatively old age of seventy-three. The physician he sought treatment from in Halle, Johann Christian Reil, diagnosed him with 'atony of the heart muscle' – though, as Ann Schmiesing notes, his diagnosis has since been put forth as essential parox-ysmal tachycardia, a condition in which the heartbeat accelerates to two to three times its normal rate. These episodes can last from several minutes to several hours and are accompanied by dizziness and light-headedness, a condition that greatly affected Wilhelm's ability to function in his daily life.

At Halle, Reil prescribed a litany of treatments, including electric shock therapy, magnet therapy, and an assortment of pills. In his letters to his brother, Wilhelm showed himself to be both frightened of his treatments – the electric shock ther-apy made his skin blister – and grateful for the fact that, effec-tive or not, they allowed him to sleep once more at night. 'I feel of course,' he writes in a letter dated August 1809, 'that I cannot be fully helped, and that I must die of it, but I am thankful to God with all of my heart for this improvement, under which I can live and work peacefully and with joy.'

Wilhelm returned to live with his brother after this treat-ment, and it is perhaps not surprising that many of the subse-quent editions and revisions to the KHM have increased mentions of disability. After the first two volumes of the *KHM* were published in 1812 and 1815, Wilhelm assumed more responsibility for editing subsequent versions, and under his editorial hand the prevalence of disability throughout the tales – sixteen more versions of which were published from 1819 to 1858 – increased. This *narrative prosthesis* – wherein the narratives are added to and supplemented by additional character traits – infiltrates all subsequent editions of the text.

This increase in disabled characteristics and features in the tales is likely due not so much to Wilhelm Grimm's desire to reflect the world – though disability was, in the eighteenth and nineteenth centuries, certainly more of a *visible* fact of life due to the prevalence of many crippling diseases and conditions (polio, smallpox, scarlet fever, cholera, to name a few examples) for which there was no cure – as much as it was due to his sense of wanting to restore the tales and make them 'complete.'

This 'completeness,' in turn, has much to do with what folk-tale scholar Vladimir Propp identified as the 'lack-lack-liquidation pattern' in folk-tale narratives. Essentially, the lack-lack-liquidation pattern highlights the way in which a tale starts out with a need or want on the part of the narrator (the desire for something that is *lacking*) and then moves through to the liquidation of that desire through fulfilment of the quest. In his *Morphology of the Folk Tale*, published in Russia in 1928, Propp outlines how the lack-lack-liquidation pattern moves from uncertainty to balance – essentially from struggle to triumph – so that the story might feel complete. Or, as Schmiesing puts it: '[the lack-lack-liquidation pattern] moves from disequilibrium to equilibrium, from disenchantment to enchantment, and from disability to ability and bodily perfection.'

The later insertion of disability into the Grimms' tales increased the narrative arc of their stories, putting the protagonists at an increased disadvantage at the outset, giving them more to gain through the successful completion of their quests. The Maiden Without Hands is rewarded doubly at the end of her tale by virtue of having her hands grow back. Likewise, the ostracization of Hans My Hedgehog is made that much more severe and cruel due to the non-human nature of his disfigurement. He is quite literally transformed, at the end, from an animal into a human; had he been born a 'normal' boy, the tale itself would not have had the same journey, the same *Naturpoesie* heart and triumph over adversity that the Grimms were so determined to uphold.

Disability in the Grimm tales also operated as a way of further entrenching the characters of the tales and making them unforgettable. In the original version of 'Old Sultan,' a tale about a farmer and his faithful dog, the dog has no disability. In subsequent versions the dog is described as 'toothless,' and thus becomes all the more memorable. Healthy dogs are a dime a dozen; you remember the toothless dog, though, whether or not you're repulsed by it.

In *Disability Aesthetics*, Tobin Siebers notes that modern art's move away from traditionally classical forms – and the subsequent celebration of modernist palettes and the disabilities and so-called 'flaws' in the human body — is, in fact, the very thing that allows art to transcend time and memory. (In *Les Menottes de cuivre*, René Magritte's revisioning of the Venus de Milo, for example, red pigment is splashed on the arm stumps of the Venus de Milo to give the impression of a recent and painful amputation.) 'It is often the presence of disability that allows the beauty of an artwork to endure over time,' writes Siebers.

It is, in effect, easy to forget a blandly beautiful human body. It is much harder to forget the body that arrests, the body that is different from the norm.

You don't forget the man who has a hedgehog's upper body, or the woman who has no hands. And chances are you'll forever remember the writer who told that story to you, too.

I start writing stories when I'm five years old. This is also, like the dress I wear when I leave the hospital after my first surgery, something that makes me feel special. I write stories about animals: about my family dog, about birds, about dinosaurs. In Grade 1, I write a story about a rabbit and glue cotton balls to all of my rabbit illustrations. I write stories about my family and about owls and about love. I write a story about the boy I have a crush on – at the end of the story, we get married. (I still don't really understand what marriage means, but I draw myself wearing a beautiful white dress at the wedding.) One year, for Thanksgiving, I write a story on special paper that's cut in the shape of a turkey.

I write about princesses. If they are not already beautiful (mostly they are), they are always made beautiful by the end of the story. They have *raven-dark* hair or *golden-blond* hair and their eyes are never anything but blue. They are always kind, even when those around them don't deserve it.

I never write stories about princesses in wheelchairs, or princesses who have to hang their legs out of the tub when they're taking a bath. I don't write about girls who have crutches. I don't write about girls who are told they are ugly because they walk differently than everyone else. I don't write stories that don't have happy endings.

I am five, then six. My mother reads us *The Swiss Family Robinson* and *Anne of Green Gables* and books about Clifford the Big Red Dog. No one is disabled in any of these stories, not that I notice at the time.

After I get out of the hospital for my second surgery, the one that gives me a cast, I read the *Little House* books from beginning to end again. Mary Ingalls has scarlet fever and loses the sight in both her eyes. She is still beautiful and blond and good – like a princess, only not a fairy-tale one. Ma Ingalls and Laura make her a trousseau when she travels away to the school for the blind. They make her a beautiful gown of rich brown cashmere. She is blind, but she has Laura to guide her through the world and then, when at school, she learns to be more independent.

I don't see her as disabled when I read the novel as a girl. The only disabled people I know of have canes or use wheelchairs. Eventually I don't have either of those things anymore, so I don't see myself as disabled either. I can walk like the princesses in the stories I read.

I can't wear their shoes, though. No matter how I try.

In subsequent editions of their work, the Brothers Grimm also made more than a few editorial adjustments in response to complaints about the stories not being suitable for children. The burgeoning middle class in Germany and other countries meant both a growing literate population and, as the population shifted slowly and inexorably toward cities and away from the work cycle of growing up on a farm, an increased focus on childhood and what did and did not constitute 'acceptable' points of focus in child-rearing.

The Grimms were raised as Calvinists, and their strict adherence to their faith permeates many aspects of their tales, particularly with regard to gender roles – it's no surprise, then, to discover that even their disabled protagonists are expected to act and behave in ways befitting the religious beliefs around gender roles at the time. Hans My Hedgehog is *allowed* to be forthright and loud about his disability in a way that the Maiden Without Hands is not. He is allowed to demand things of his father, of his town, whereas the Maiden refuses her father's help and casts herself out into society instead. It is arguably because of her meekness and her acquiescence to power (God) that her hands grow back in the end, whereas Hans My Hedgehog gains his comely human form through use of his own cunning. There are lessons here that even the youngest of children can learn.

It's important to remember that the Napoleonic wars were in full swing when the *KHM* was first published, and parts of Germany were occupied by France. Some of the revisions made to subsequent editions of the tales involved removing mentions of France and allusions to things traditionally associated with French culture; further additions and embellishments were made in the interest of boosting German nationalism. (Thus the removal, in many of the tales, of fairy godmothers, replaced instead by God and other patriarchal figures suitable to German tastes of the time.) A suite of German stories made gentle for children offered a perfect way to subtly instruct a populace on the ways to be a good German, to be good boys and girls in the world. The princess in 'The Frog King' is admonished by her father for being rude to the frog that has retrieved her beloved golden ball from the well ('You must keep your promise, no matter what you said'). She is disgusted by the frog, slimy and *other* as he is, but she does as she's told because she's a good daughter. And what does she get in return? A handsome prince, and a love story to last the ages.

But no one believes bedtime stories, you say. *Those are only for children. We know they aren't real.*

The Nazis were also interested in the German *Naturpoesie*, as we now know. They believed in the unifying power of story for the German people, and, like the Grimms, in the freshness and the power and the *purity* of the German countryside – as opposed to the cities, places where vermin ran, places where all kinds of unsavoury characters – and races – might mingle. It isn't a stretch to draw a line from the Grimms' treatment of stories and storytelling as a nationalistic device through to Nazi Germany and the depiction of the disabled, othered body as something that needs to be extinguished.

There were no fairy godmothers in Nazi Germany, no benevolent strangers waiting to bless a mutilated body so its hands might grow back. There were only those who saw an ideal of the human body – the muscular German male so lionized in Nazi propaganda art, the female with her ample breasts and healthy hips. There were only the stories of the disabled-as-other that so many believed, and would continue to believe as the tales were told and retold – before bedtime, before the nighttime fire. Rumpelstiltskin the evil dwarf. The stepsisters of Aschenputtel, the Grimms' version of Cinderella, who willingly cut off their toes and parts of their feet so they might fit into the glass slipper and thereby win the prince. The deformed body giving face to the deformed heart – first in stories told for adults, then in stories told for children, then in stories repackaged and repurposed and told for adults again on posters and in film, broadcast across a country.

Fairy stories are not real, no. But neither are they ever *only stories*.

For most of my nine years in elementary school, I have a crush on a boy who we'll call John. John is an athlete, and I am not. He is popular, and I am not. He says maybe fifteen words to me the entire time we're in school together. I watch him on the playground every day; I steal furtive glances at him when we sit in class. He isn't mean to me, not exactly, but it's quite clear that he couldn't care less that I'm alive.

In Grade 4 – we are nine – he starts dating the new girl in class. Her name is Grace. (This is also not her real name, but what better name for her than one that belonged to a real princess?) She is small and blond and dainty. She is also not mean to me, not exactly, but I do not belong to the popular circles, and she fits in there right away. I walk funny, I get my breasts and my period before everyone else. I have half-frizzy, half-scraggly straight hair that never knows what to do. My eyebrows are huge caterpillars. When I look at photos of myself, I know that I am not the kind of girl that anyone could love.

I am wrong about this, which I realize years later, looking back over all of those photos from school. The pictures show a shy young girl with a hesitant smile and brown eyes that gleam when you ask her to tell you a story. My head tilts ever so slightly to the left in almost all of my pictures. I see this now all the time – back then, I noticed it only at the hairdresser, when the stylist would continually straighten my lopsided head in the mirror, and also sometimes at school, when the other kids around me would tilt their heads and I was never sure if they were mocking me or not.

I grow up fantasizing about ballet shoes, leotards, the theatre stage. When I am twelve and enrolled in figure skating lessons, I choreograph an imaginary routine to the soundtrack from *The Lion King*. I close my bedroom door and twirl alone for hours in the centre of the carpet.

But the realities of dance class and figure skating are very different. My feet are stiff, my hip bones lopsided, my right leg two inches shorter than my left. My spine is curved by the whisper of scoliosis – a side effect of the cerebral palsy, along with increased likelihood of any or all of the following: early adult-onset arthritis, tendonitis, excessive fatigue as one grows older, and constant pain. Hands and feet that know what I want them to do but will not always do it. Thighs given to trembling. Knees given to spasms. An imagination that goes everywhere. A body that will not always follow.

I do not grow up in a time and place with Nazi posters, or with the overt idea that the disabled body is bad. (The disabled body is not really talked about, as such, in school or out in the world.) What I have, instead, are brightly coloured VHS tapes with soft edges. A mermaid princess with red hair and a purple seashell bra; a brown-eyed French brunette who loves books and swings like Tarzan from the moving ladders of her library. A black-haired Arabian princess who falls in love with a street urchin and journeys with him on a magic carpet; an Indigenous princess, tall and statuesque, who runs barefoot through the forest without a single thought of stumbling. A blond-haired, blue-eyed princess who is tricked into touching a spindle and falls into a deep sleep but is rescued by her love and able to dance triumphantly at the end of the tale, her princess's dress plunging from pink to blue and back again. A Black princess who kisses a frog and changes her life. Princess meets prince and falls in love, over and over and over again.

And I have Quasimodo, misshapen and kind, who finds friends at the end of his story and is happy about it, because that is the only kind of happiness he is allowed to have.

4

Someday My Prince Will Come:
Disney and the World Without Shadows

Fairy tales continued to grow in popularity throughout Europe over the course of the nineteenth and early-twentieth centuries. In Denmark, Hans Christian Andersen was writing about his Little Mermaid, his Ugly Duckling, and his Emperor with New Clothes; in England there were Jack and the Beanstalk, Goldilocks, and the Three Little Pigs. With the advent of the twentieth century and the slow rise of the United States as a storytelling power came L. Frank Baum and *The Wonderful Wizard of Oz* – a story about a group of motley, arguably disabled characters (no heart, no brain, no courage) who banded together and made their way through a strange new land in search of wholeness.

In California, a man named Walt Disney began an animation studio, the Disney Brothers Cartoon Studio, in 1923. In conjunction with his business partner and brother, Roy Disney, Walt built an animation empire that would eventually transform the world.

Before setting up in California, Disney had made a series of shorts called Laugh-O-Grams while working for a Kansas City advertising company. One of these told a modern version of Cinderella that sees our heroine scrubbing dishes in a kitchen with her only friend the cat. (In this black-and-white version there is no pumpkin and no mice – the fairy godmother instead transforms empty air in front of Cinderella into a Ford Model T and decks her out in a flapper's dress and beads. At the end, the stepsisters aren't mutilated – only lonely and miserable.) It was in Kansas that he also made his first film employing both animation and live-action techniques: a short starring four-year-old Virginia Davis based on *Alice in Wonderland*.

(Disney, it should be noted, was influenced by the works of cartoonist Paul Terry, who created and produced the *Aesop's Fables* series of animated shorts under his company Fables Studios. The series launched with *The Goose That Laid the Golden Egg* in 1921 and continued under the Fables name until 1929, when Terry left the company. The remaining shorts in the series were completed under the Van Beuren Studios and ran until 1936.)

In California, Disney moved on to creating the character of Oswald the Lucky Rabbit, an adventurous rabbit who already espoused the physical ideals that would be woven through Disney's later films (Disney wanted the rabbit to be 'peppy, alert, saucy and venturesome, keeping him also neat and trim'). A dispute over intellectual property rights to Oswald led to the abandonment of that character and the creation of the iconic Mickey Mouse in 1928 – a character that became so successful so quickly that it led to Disney being awarded an honorary Oscar for the creation of Mickey in 1932.

But Disney had bigger dreams. Specifically, he thought that full-length films offered more opportunities for animation – and with his fairy-tale training and knowledge behind him, he set out to remake the world.

In a way, this book begins here, because I also begin here. I begin with Disney in the theatre – the giant plush seats and my seven-year-old body folding into them, the way that I wasn't big enough to keep the seat down all the way and so always sat in a slight upward V-shape.

I begin with Disney as a video release on VHS – the bulky smoothness of the tape, the way the TV screen wiggles when we rewind the tapes over and over again to our favourite parts.

I begin with *One Hundred and One Dalmatians* on an Easter morning when I'm ten. Whenever I see that film now I think of chocolate.

I begin with *Beauty and the Beast*, with *The Rescuers*, with Miss Bianca and Bernard the mouse in their original adventure, helping orphan Penny as she's lifted down into the mine.

I begin with Jasmine and Aladdin, with Simba the Lion King, with beautiful Aurora and her magical, colour-shifting dress. I begin, over and over, with Ariel the Little Mermaid who sings under the sea.

I begin with Disney.

The 'Disneyfication' of well-known fairy tales – wherein the happy endings became even happier, and the darker elements of traditional tales were passed over in favour of less controversial storylines – became a hallmark of the twentieth century starting in 1937, with the release of Disney's first full-length animated feature, *Snow White and the Seven Dwarfs*. Walt Disney, who knew the original tale by the Brothers Grimm, felt that the tale had potential to fill out a feature-length animated film. In particular, Disney thought a great deal of comic relief could be had from the personalities of the dwarfs, who had not been named in the Brothers Grimm version of the tale and offered, Disney felt, a wealth of opportunity for the studio to expand and further endear the story to a modern audience.

And so: Happy, Sneezy, Grumpy, Bashful, Sleepy, Dopey, and Doc. Seven dwarfs to make fun of, seven dwarfs to counterbalance the princess and the prince and the evil, scheming queen. Seven bright faces to blot out the darkness. Seven different bodies to distract us from what's lurking in the healthy ones.

It worked, as a strategy. *Snow White and the Seven Dwarfs* cost almost US$1.5 million to make – well over the original budget of $250,000. The film grossed nearly $8 million worldwide in its first run. Proceeds from the film allowed Walt Disney to build new studios in Burbank, California, and within a year of the film's premiere, plans were already underway for Disney's next two animated feature films, *Fantasia* and *Pinocchio*, with other well-known tales – *Peter Pan, Dumbo, Alice in Wonderland* – soon to follow. *Cinderella* came in 1950, with *Sleeping Beauty* appearing in 1959. Nods to other European fairy and folk tales slowly appeared with films like *Robin Hood* (1973) and *The Little Mermaid* (1989); storytelling expanded to other continents with *Aladdin* (1992), *The Lion King* (1994), and *Mulan* (1998).

Storylines for the films were culled from cultures all over the world and pressed into a tried-and-true formula: plucky hero/heroine, quest, loyal sidekick often used for laughs. There was usually a broken family of some kind – one or more dead parents (*Snow White, Bambi, Aladdin, The Little Mermaid, The Rescuers, Cinderella, Beauty and the Beast* ...) and some element of ostracization of the main character through no fault of their own. (Belle in *Beauty and the Beast* is seen as eccentric because she loves to read; Ariel in *The Little Mermaid* is set apart from her fellow mermaids and mermen because of her fascination with the world above the sea; Jasmine in *Aladdin* is set up as a maverick because she does not want to go through with an arranged royal marriage; Aladdin himself is a street orphan and social outcast – even the Genie, arguably, is an outcast, kept as he is from the world due to the confines of his lamp.)

There was also generally some element of disability in the films that was played up for comic or tragic effect. Snow White had her dwarfs; Pinocchio had his nose; even Sleeping Beauty had a condition, magically bestowed though it was, that kept her apart from the world. Ariel could not walk for the first half of her film, though it was true she could move in other ways. Quasimodo, the lovable Hunchback of Notre Dame, was ostracized in his bell tower. Scar, the villain in *The Lion King*, was so closely associated with his disability and disfigurement that he didn't even have a separate name.

I didn't notice any of this when I was a child – or, at least, I didn't notice it outright. I noticed it in the way that children always notice things – faithfully, unquestioningly – content to let the world I saw on television build the world I saw outside, even though I didn't realize it at the time.

I came of age just before Disney expanded its franchise in several crucial ways. I was thirteen years old the year the Disney Store opened in my local mall. I never went to Disneyworld or Disneyland. Because my world wasn't inundated with Disney merchandise or trips, the tales I saw onscreen mostly remained stories – stories my siblings and I were happy to act out in our backyard, yes, but stories all the same. The world of Disney merchandise – and, arguably, the world of Disney we all now know and see – had not yet become quite a *thing*.

But still, the lessons were there. You don't watch *The Little Mermaid* hundreds of times without learning a few crucial things: how important walking is, the desperate measures one might take to be with the person they love. What is and is not *acceptable* in polite society. Ariel walked toward her happiness in the end. Pinocchio's happy ending came with a nose that was 'normal.' Quasimodo had friends at the end of his tale but he didn't have romantic love. After all, how could he? Would Quasimodo fit in a Disney Princes line of merchandise if ever there was such a thing? Wouldn't he spoil the effect, sticking out as he does in a line of princes all so bland and boring?

And Scar, the erstwhile villain who embodies disfigurement of both the body and soul? He dies in the end, eradicated in the way that all true evil should be.

Except it isn't evil, really. Scar as a character is second in line to the throne, condemned to live in his older brother's larger, more powerful shadow. (His original name was Taka, which means 'dirt' or 'filth' in Swahili. As legend has it, he took the name Scar to remind himself that jealousy and hate almost cost him an eye – but Jealousy doesn't have as much of an impact as a name, does it?)

Who's to say that the Beast in *Beauty and the Beast* isn't made precisely as terrible as he is as a result of the world's reaction to his disfigurement? It is the world's shunning that causes so much of the problem – the social ills that Hans My Hedgehog so determinedly pushed against, the social pressures that made the princess Mama recognize herself as inferior and choose intelligence at whatever cost. The world did this.

The world *does* this.

But what's the big deal? everyone says again. *Everyone knows that Disney movies aren't real.*
It's just a movie.

Grow up.
Get over it.

'Remove imperfection from the body,' says Tobin Siebers, 'and one discovers the perfect recipe for what does not exist for the most part in the human universe.'

This is a paradox at once unique to both human nature and fairy tales. You cannot reach for a better society without recognizing that the society in which you live is also itself imperfect – the two go hand in hand. So if you're going to tell an idealized story about a father who wishes for a child or a princess who wishes for intelligence or a son who wishes to go out and seek his fortune in the world, and if the fulfillment of that quest symbolizes perfection, the *here and now* of the characters themselves must somehow show the flaws through which they begin to shape their quest.

And what better, faster, easier way for a storyteller to show this so-called imperfection than through the metaphor of disability, an idea that is already so ingrained in society as emblematic of the imperfect?

I hear so many stories from disabled women and men who used to be little disabled girls and boys. The stories all hurt in the same way.

I was never there in fairy tales. I never saw myself.

I saw myself, but I was always the bad guy. You never get to be the princess when you look different.

There's the story of Irené Colthurst, who like me has cerebral palsy and as a young girl watched Cinderella put her foot into a glass slipper. Irené got her shoes from Nordstrom, the only store that allowed you to mix and match shoes of the same style but different sizes. 'Some of the most unpleasant memories I have,' she tells me, 'are of sitting in the shoe depart-ment ... the shoes rubbed so much that they could and often did rub sores in my feet. Sometimes to the point of bleeding.'

But Cinderella, Irené notes, never had trouble like this. 'Nobody else fits into the dainty-foot shoe, and this is how easily she slips back into it? *Voila, happily ever after?*'

The story of Dominick Evans, a disabled trans filmmaker, who never saw himself in these stories growing up. 'I wasn't a pretty little girl,' he remembers. 'And all of those stories were about pretty little girls – never mind trans or disabled characters!'

The story of Sarah Jama, a Somali-Canadian disability organizer and co-founder of the Disability Justice Network of Ontario, who identified with the heroes in fairy tales because she was afraid to identify as the princess and the damsel-in-distress. 'As a disabled immigrant, you can't be weak, because weakness then translates into being a burden on the system.'

What messages do we internalize, as disabled children, when we see a world that looks so easy on the screen and then struggle with the world in real life?

'If you get seven little people together in a car or an elevator,' Rebecca Cokley tells me, 'you can bet we're going to make jokes about it. But that's an entirely different thing from some-one who is not a little person making the same jokes.'

Rebecca Cokley is the Senior Fellow for Disability Policy at the Center for American Progress. I speak with her in mid-February of 2019, a few weeks after President Donald Trump delivers his State of the Union address.

'He mentioned the disabled in his speech,' she notes, smil-ing faintly at the irony. 'I worked for Obama for nearly ten years and we were never able to get the disabled in the State of the Union. So at least it's there, I guess.'

Rebecca has achondroplasia, a common cause of dwarfism. She's a second-generation little person – her parents met at a Little People of America convention in the 1970s. Growing up as a little person in a family of little people, she felt acutely aware both of how little people are portrayed in fairy-tale culture – from Rumpelstiltskin to the Seven Dwarfs, from Thumbelina to Tinker Bell – and how she did not fit into that idea. 'You'll find in many cases where there's average-height parents who have children who are little people, they spend a lot of time trying to protect their kids from that kind of stuff,' she explains. 'But when the parents and kids are little people, we have no problem understanding we're not magical creatures.' Still, it's not hard for Rebecca to see how disability runs as a narrative through most fairy tales – and from there, how it runs as a narrative in our stories, political, fantastical, and otherwise, today. It is, after all, such an easy way to show how someone is different.

Do you remember that version of 'Hansel and Gretel' where the witch comes to the door with a crutch and then cooks and eats the children? Rebecca does, for sure. 'When you look at these stories,' she says, 'how they were written, what was thought about disability in those times – stories are one of those constructs that have the most power because they get you at such a young age.'

And while times might have changed, when it comes to the films of Disney, certain things have remained the same. The unmistakably evil sorceress, the stepmother, the sharpness of Jafar's face in *Aladdin*. The slash across the face of Scar.

The princesses, beautiful and true. Red-haired and black-haired and blond-haired and brown. Funny and independent and so quick to fall in love. For several of them, *sixteen years old* when they fall in love and win their princes.

It took seventy-two years for Disney to make a film starring a Black princess. Fifty-five years for a princess who was South Asian. Fifty-eight years for an Indigenous princess. Sixty-one years for a princess from China.

No disabled princess yet, so far as I can see.

It's important here to stop and recognize one crucial thing. Fairy tales exist in different forms all over the world. And yet despite their differences, there have been similarities found between many tales of different cultures – similarities so striking that they drove the creation of the Aarne-Thompson-Uther Index, a method of cataloguing various fairy tales from across the world. The ATU was developed in Finland by Antti Aarne in the early twentieth century and subsequently modified by the American folklorist Stith Thompson and German folklorist Hans-Jörg Uther in 1928 and 2004, respectively. It comprises a vast database where all of the fairy-tale motifs we know and love are catalogued together – the stepmother, the boy or girl who makes their way out into the world, the friendly stranger, the animal helper, the 'rule of three' (Goldilocks and the Three Bears, the Three Little Pigs). Time and time again, one can root through the ATU and see similar themes popping up in tales told on opposite sides of the globe.

Well, you say, *that's hardly surprising, is it? Stories, after all, are universal.*

Except that they aren't, not wholly. Stories as we know them are inextricably bound up in the social and societal expectations of the cultures in which they arise – they arise *because* of a culture, not in spite of it. And so the plucky girl or boy who defies their parents and sets out to make their fortune speaks to a universal experience not simply because the desire to go out into the world is universal, but because the *societies* that keep these boys or girls back – whether through patriarchy, income disparity, barriers to the disabled, or some other means – are themselves the overarching universalities that hold us all together.

The evil stepmother is a fixture in European fairy tales because the stepmother was very much a fixture in early European society – mortality in childbirth was very high, and it wasn't unusual for a father to suddenly find himself alone with multiple mouths to feed. So he remarried and brought another woman into the house, and eventually they had yet more children, thus changing the power dynamics of inheritance in the household in a way that had very little to do with inherent, archetypal evil and everything to do with social expectation and pressure. What was a woman to do when she remarried into a family and had to act as mother to her husband's children as well as her own, in a time when economic prosperity was a magical dream for most? Would she think of killing her husband's children so that her own children might therefore inherit and thrive? Would she argue, like the stepmother does in 'Hansel and Gretel,' that the children must leave the house in order for the husband and his wife to survive? Perhaps. Perhaps not. But the *fear* that stepmothers (or stepfathers) might do this kind of thing was very real, and it was that fear – fed by the socioeconomic pressures felt by the growing urban class – that fed the stories.

We see this also with the stories passed around in France – fairies who swoop in to save the day when women themselves can't do so; romantic tales of young girls who marry beasts as a balm to those young ladies facing arranged marriages to older, distant dukes. We see this with the removal of fairies and insertion of religion into the German tales.

Fairy tales, in short, are not created in a vacuum. As with all stories, they change and bend both with and in response to culture. And Disney knew this.

'There's a real kind of connectedness and savviness to the way that Disney told tales,' author and scholar Sarah Henstra tells me. We speak in Toronto on a bright day in March, as the last vestiges of winter are gathering themselves on the wind. Sarah teaches a course at Ryerson University called 'Fairy Tales and Fantasies.' In it, she introduces students to the archetypes that permeate most of the fairy tales we know in the Western world – as well as the countless spinoffs, revisionings, and interpretations of these tales that make their way into mainstream Western media.

'It's not like Disney went in with some nefarious agenda to make everything saccharine and palatable – he was trying to fill the movie house. Fairy tales are always a product of the cultural preoccupations of the time,' Sarah says. 'Even Snow White herself, in the film – she's always talking about attitude adjustments. Audiences in the 1930s needed to hear something more than "grit and positive thinking will pull you through," something packaged differently, because at the time, nothing else was working.'

It's no coincidence, in other words, that Disney chose Snow White – a magical princess, displayed on a screen with new technology that has its audience instantly enamoured – to exhort the dwarfs to *whistle while you work*, encouraging her gruff and humble new friends to find what joy they could in a hardscrabble, earthy existence. It's one thing to hear this from the government or other sources of power – it's another thing entirely to be romanced into the thinking via a cinematic experience unlike any other. In 1937 the Great Depression had tumbled back into a recession and the need for both escape and encouragement was high. What better way to bring magic back into the world than through story, packaged in a way no one had quite seen before? What better way to encourage people to be cheerful and optimistic than through a beautiful princess who continues to smile and dance despite the darkness in her life?

(It's also no coincidence that there's a fetishization of the dwarfs as a kind of earthy, 'common' folk – in their cheerfulness and willingness to take in a stranger and share what resources they have, one can see echoes of both the charity model [*be kind, do good, do unto others*] and the condescension therein – *look at these cheerful dwarfs, doing so much with so little!* – as well as the communism that was stirring in opposition to fascist regimes on the rise in other parts of the world. Was it intentional, the connecting of these othered individuals to the values of humility and collective good – values that would eventually come to be demonized in their own way, associated with a negative kind of simplicity and otherness once again? Perhaps not consciously, but the drawing of those lines was still pronounced. Snow White is different from the dwarfs – she can learn from them, as they can from her, but at the end of the day they are still different people. They have their humble cottage, and she goes on to live in a castle.)

'There's this pattern that we map onto fairy tales and mythology,' Sarah notes. 'You have a landscape strewn with obstacles, a chosen or unchosen hero – someone who refuses the call and then follows. There is often a magical helper who sees to it that the hero goes out into the open world, into the space of adventure. If it's a female protagonist, there tends to be a moment of disobedience, or a moment of disruption that leads to a bad bargain, and from there the need for the protagonist to overcome these obstacles and triumph.'

The Maiden Without Hands is the result of a bad bargain, when her father unwittingly turns her over to the Devil, thinking he's only given away his apple tree. In Disney's *The Little Mermaid*, Ariel makes her own bad bargain with Ursula the Sea Witch; in Disney's *Sleeping Beauty*, the parents of Princess Aurora make an arguably bad bargain with the fairies to protect her from harm; in Disney's *Cinderella*, the bargain struck with the fairy godmother is perhaps not as bad as some but still makes for difficulty when the clock strikes twelve. The young Tahitian princess Moana learns the hard way what it means to cast oneself away from the comforts of home on the fairy-tale quest. And yet, as their narratives cycle through to completion, all of these female narrators manage to triumph. Slowly, subtly, Disney has managed over the years to champion the virtues of independence and strength – as well as kindness and beauty – in a way that's perhaps not as overtly political as the indestructible cheerfulness of Snow White but every bit as powerful.

What does it mean, though, to champion an independence that looks and talks and *walks* a very certain, particular way? To imaginatively respond to cultural pressures and change and yet manage to stay immobile and still when it comes to depictions of the disabled body? As a young girl growing up with a wheelchair, then crutches, then a limp, what does it mean to watch a princess put her foot into a glass slipper and understand that this glass slipper holds all promises of her dreams come true?

What happens when you know that your own foot would never fit in a slipper like that, much less be good for dancing?

The Disney Princesses, as most families and young children know them today, became a brand in 2000, after Disney executive Andy Mooney attended a showing of *Disney on Ice* and noticed that young girls were dressed up in bespoke princess costumes at the event. Inspired by the possibilities for commercial expansion, Mooney returned to his Disney office and ordered his creative team to start thinking about merchandise geared specifically around the most well-known princesses in the Disney movie line.

The line grossed $300 million in its first year; by 2012, annual revenue was over $3 billion. The line started with Snow White, Cinderella, Aurora, Ariel, Belle, Jasmine, Pocahontas, Mulan, and Tinker Bell, but Tinker Bell left the line shortly after inception to head the Disney Fairies. Tiana, the African-American main character in *The Princess and the Frog*, took over Tinker Bell's spot in 2010; in 2011, Rapunzel joined the lot. The eleventh member, *Brave*'s Scottish princess Merida, joined the franchise in 2013.

It's a line of princesses who are at once all different and yet entirely the same – all young, all beautiful. Mostly white. Four women of colour. They have open smiles and bright, trusting natures. With the exception of Merida, they all find love – but then Merida isn't really looking for love, so love doesn't matter.

Together, they sing the same song, over and over: be kind, be bold, be true. Whistle while you work and have faith in your dreams and, as Cinderella sang, *'someday your rainbow will come smiling through.'* Ask for adventure, ask for love. Trust in yourself and your story and happily ever after will be yours, too.

This is also a political message, positive and pure though it might seem. It assumes a whole manner of things that go unsaid: beauty; a largely heteronormative approach to romance; the privilege of resources and pluck. (We aren't all of us able to wrest a future from hardscrabble origins, nor are most of us the lucky recipients of a fairy godmother's love.) From a feminist perspective, the Disney Princesses champion female empowerment while also drawing that empowerment clearly within the lines of *adjacency* to male privilege and power – even bow-slinging, bear-tussling Merida, singular as she is, proves her worth in part because she's *just as good as the boys*.

Most importantly, it's a message that assumes absolute and unrealistic able-bodiedness. No one with glasses. No crutches, no wheelchairs, no visible differences from girl to girl apart from the colour of their eyes and hair. Perfectly symmetrical faces abound. Some of the princesses – Mulan and Merida in particular – are athletes, with the kind of unrealistic body control and power that even able-bodied people often struggle to obtain. The message is that heroism isn't possible without physical 'perfection,' especially for girls.

(This longing for perfection in the form of physical prowess is so insidious that it pervades even the way we think about disability; disabled people who can achieve some measure of physical participation in sport are inevitably placed higher on the physical hierarchy than those who cannot, leading to the dichotomy of the 'super-crip' narrative, where the disabled athlete is seen as more powerful than their non-athletic disabled brethren. In actuality, the issue is not that some disabled people are more capable than others and thus more worthy of consideration in the realm of sport, but that sport is not adapted on a wider level and made accessible to all disabled people.

When it comes to Mulan in particular, the aspect of the title character being marginalized as a result of her 'inferior' female body raises an interesting question. Disability, notes Siebers, '[has] served to justify oppression by amplifying ideas about inferiority already attached to other minority identities.' The scholar Talila A. Lewis expands on this in her working definition of ableism available on her website – a working definition, she notes, that is grounded in community work and conversation:

> Ableism is a system that places value on people's bodies and minds based on societally constructed ideas of normalcy, intelligence, and excellence. These constructed ideas of normalcy, intelligence, and excellence are deeply rooted in anti-Blackness, eugenics, and capitalism.
>
> This form of systemic oppression leads to people and society determining who is valuable and worthy based on people's appearance and/or their ability to satisfactorily produce, excel, and 'behave.'

Under this definition of ableism, it is possible to see how Mulan, perceived as inferior through dint of her female body, could be seen to have experienced ableism. In the film, she overcomes others' perceptions of her as unworthy by proving that she is, indeed, just as good or even better than any man who has enlisted in the army alongside her – in short, she triumphs not by getting others to recognize that her own different body is just as valuable as the next, but by making her body fit a constructed idea of what it means to be productive and valuable in society. She is not valuable until she is the same as everyone else.)

The spell of sameness can only be broken, it seems, by the villains. Differences, when we find them in Disney, lie not with the princesses but with their antagonists – the sorceress, the evil witch, the stepmother. A crooked nose and green skin and horns, and we know, instantly, who we have to root for, and who must be defeated.

When Rebecca Cokley was young, one of her favourite parts of fairy tales were the villains. She loved Maleficent, in the original animated Disney version of *Sleeping Beauty*, in particular – how striking she was, how different from those around her. Her green skin, her horns, her pointed chin, and wings. 'She carried herself,' she tells me, 'with such confidence and power.'

Errol Kerr, based in Newcastle in the UK, tells me much the same. He was diagnosed with autism at the age of six, and then diagnosed with hypermobility syndrome at fifteen. Like Rebecca, he grew up with stories – in his case, with a father who read to him from all manner of fantasy and fairy-tale stories, from *The Lord of the Rings* through to *Dune* through to the Brothers Grimm. And as a child of the nineties, he was exposed to all things Disney and found the narratives comforting in their familiarity. It's a familiarity and comfort that he recognizes as problematic now, but still the nostalgia remains.

'The 2014 film' – *Maleficent*, with Angelina Jolie – 'took the Sleeping Beauty story in a direction I was afraid it wouldn't have the guts to do,' he says. 'Particularly with regard to the forcible removal of a particular kind of mobility as tantamount to rape. I think that's definitely something that can and should be discussed more.'

(In *Maleficent*, it is Maleficent herself who is violated when she is drugged, and her fairy wings are taken from her by her old friend Stefan. But as we will see in Chapter Seven, the spectre of rape in 'Sleeping Beauty' is actually a very old part of the story.)

Errol studied at Newcastle University and sits on the executive committee of Autistic UK. Like me, like Rebecca, he's a Disney fan of the *it's complicated* variety. He is skeptical, for example, that the planned live-action remake of *The Hunchback of Notre Dame* will bring any particular gains.

'Other than *Maleficent*, all of the films that Disney is currently making appear to be identical to their animated versions,' he says. 'And the Disney version of *The Hunchback of Notre Dame* was very family-friendly, pitiful inspiration porn.' He doesn't see much hope for growth and inclusion with regard to disability in retellings like these, and we are both agreed on this: for fairy tales to keep their power as we move into the twenty-first century, growth and change are essential.

Essential because the nostalgia that keeps drawing us back to the brightness of Disney films and their ilk also has its dark underpinnings. Like the nostalgia that the Grimms evoked for the bygone paradise of rural German life (a paradise that was itself non-existent, as it doesn't take a historian to recognize how difficult life was for the peasantry), it's a nostalgia that yearns for a time that *never actually was*. There was never a time when magic ruled the world; there was never a time when plucky Jack could climb a beanstalk and defeat the giant, upending the social order. Even in the story of 'Jack and the Beanstalk' itself, the triumph is contained – it's only Jack and his mother who are well-fed at the end of the tale. Society, as we have seen, does not change in fairy tales. The transformation is individual, never systemic.

So, too, with Disney. Transformation is all well and good, but if it's only an individual who changes, what does that mean for society at large? What does it mean for a young, physically disabled girl who might dream about being a princess to also know, at the same time, that the wider world doesn't believe in a princess who might use a wheelchair – but is more than ready to believe in a witch who uses crutches or an evil queen who transforms herself into an ugly hag?

'Fairy tales are formative pieces of work when you're a child,' Errol says. 'In my case, they established my viewpoint particularly with regard to those who have facial differences, and not in a way I'd like. I've rectified that now, but when you see as a child how the Evil Queen [in *Snow White*] uses ugliness as a disguise – and uses it as a way to *gain pity* from someone who is innocent and trusting, while we as the audience are made aware of the deception within it – that teaches you a lot, even if you're unaware of it at the time.'

One of the things it teaches a child is a sweeping – and incorrect – idea about the nature of good and evil in the world. Disney fairy tales, and many traditional fairy tales as well, operate in a world where things like good and evil are clearly defined – where the heroes and heroines are good and good-looking, kind and sweet or at the very least *likeable*, and where the villains are literally marked as such by their difference. The villains in Disney are sharp-edged and angled. Maleficent has that green skin and those wings. *Aladdin*'s Jafar is tall and thin (in contrast to the plump, kindly Sultan), while Ursula the Sea Witch has grey skin and spiked white hair and is fat, in contrast to the slender nature of Ariel and the other mermaids. Scar is physically smaller than his *Lion King* rival, Mufasa, and also painted in a paler shade; Dr. Facilier in *The Princess and the Frog* is, like Jafar, tall and thin, sharp in both personality and countenance. To look at them is to *know* that they mean harm – to understand that the darkness of their hearts is made manifest in the way they move through the world.

But navigating the world doesn't actually work this way. And while this is something we might understand on the face of it (*Obviously this isn't the real world, this is ONLY A MOVIE!*), often we internalize the fairy tale to a largely unconscious degree. Sometimes, when happy endings and obvious villains are all that you're fed, it becomes difficult to square your own experience of the world with that story. If you're shown the different body as other over and over as a child, it becomes hard to see your own different body as something that might, in turn, belong.

This goes for bodies and children of all kinds. For myself as a disabled child, it had a particular kind of staying power. Sometimes I feel like the bright colours and bright bursts of song in Disney films are as delicious and as deceptive as the witch's candy cottage hidden deep inside the woods.

You might eat, but this kind of candy will never fill you up.

Rebecca has three children now, and their experience of Disney and fairy tales is very different from the experience she had growing up. Still, so much of what she remembers has stayed the same. Two of her children are little people. All of her children are biracial, and this makes for many an interesting conversation around the Disney films they all love so much. 'My son once said to me that in Disney films, the characters are either Black or they have a disability, but they don't often have both.'

Rebecca, who is white, talks often with her children about what it means to move through the world with multiple marginalizations. Her children are still young, but already they're beginning to grasp the intricacies of a world that Disney glosses over – simply by occupying a space that's not traditionally talked about in films. 'I asked them if they thought that Elsa had a disability and my son said he'd always thought of her as having a superpower.'

(Elsa, for the uninitiated, is – along with her sister Anna – one of the heroines of *Frozen*, Disney's massively popular 2013 film about a girl [Elsa] with the power, initially uncontrollable, to manipulate the ice and snow, and the sister who saves her. It is *very loosely* based on the plot of 'The Snow Queen,' a fairy tale by Hans Christian Andersen.)

The equation of Elsa and superhero is, we can hope, telling; when it comes to Disney villains, as well as villains in mainstream media in general, Rebecca does see the beginnings of a cultural change. It's a change that has been more prevalent in the superhero stories of comic books and action movies over the last decade or so. 'The villain has an antiquated view, or doesn't understand, as opposed to them being intrinsically bad,' Rebecca says. The growing social shift – encouraged by social media movements and conversations – toward awareness and recognition of physical differences *is* beginning, however slowly, to be reflected in the stories that we tell. Perhaps we see this more in comic books because comics have had a stronger push for diverse writers and teams. Revisionings like *Maleficent* are harbingers of a change that's also happening in the fairy-tale world, but change, when it comes, is a trickle.

'It would be great to get to a point where disability isn't exotic anymore,' Rebecca says. For both of us, it's a dream and an idea that feel almost as distant as becoming a princess. Imagine: you turn on that Disney film and the protagonist picks up their cane or pulls out their wheelchair and goes off on that quest. A princess puts on her glasses, a prince gets up from his walker and calls his faithful guide-dog companion to his side. It feels revolutionary the way that fairy godmothers, in how their magic works to transform a life, feel revolutionary.

But then, fairy godmothers are everywhere in the stories we tell now. They are one of the oldest fairy-tale clichés. See how easily the magical becomes commonplace?

Would that we can all get to a point where disability feels as ordinary as a fairy godmother, too.

In my twenties, in the mid- to late-2000s, a real princess comes to the world's attention. She begins her life as Kate Middleton.

These are the stories I hold on to, which may or may not be true:

Once, when she was shopping near her family's home in Bucklebury, England, a man she'd purchased goods from asked her what he should call her. *Well, my name is Kate*, she said, smiling, *so that will do just fine*.

When she and Prince William lived in Anglesey, in Wales, she used to do all of their grocery shopping. Once, as I stood in line to buy my own groceries, I saw a tabloid photo of her pushing a shopping cart into Tesco and thought, *I will never look as beautiful dressed up as that woman does buying chicken*.

One night before they were dating, she rescued William from the unwanted attentions of another woman by slinging her arm around his neck and proclaiming him to be her boyfriend.

She wore wedge-heeled shoes a fair bit before marrying into the royal family, but doesn't that much anymore. Apparently the Queen doesn't like them.

She has a scar on her head from a surgery in childhood that you can sometimes see in photos when they're close-cropped and zoomed-in. No one in the family has ever publicly talked about it, or said what the surgery was.

Not that it matters – I'm only curious. A year or so after my own surgery at age five, another girl in my class at school had an infection that required her own shaved head and operation. I don't know the details of that either, and also wish I did. How often does this kind of thing happen to children? How many of these experiences do we get to share?

I don't know all that much else about Kate. She is married to the future king of England. They have three children and at least one dog. They live in Kensington Palace and also have a country home.

She's an amateur photographer and loves to be outdoors. Apparently, the furniture in the children's rooms all comes from IKEA.

'She knows ... that to be royal is to be yearned for, and to be yearned for is a thing to be managed,' writes Brian Phillips in his essay 'The Once and Future Queen.' '[People] will project onto you the fantasies whose reality they most long to see confirmed. They will love you if you reflect those fantasies back to them.'

She must have, I imagine, an amazing shoe collection. Other than her wedges, I've never seen her in anything other than four-inch heels. She can, and has, stood in them for hours.

My own feet have never, and will never, fit into shoes so high and pretty.

'People search for significance in the events of her youth,' writes Phillips, 'because her life looks, from the outside, like magic, and things that look like magic are easier to explain the more like magic they look.'

Of course a life only looks like magic from the outside – magic isn't real, and what looks like a fairy tale is often just an amplified version of a regular, run-of-the-mill happy story. Girl from wealthy upper-middle-class family meets boy and falls in love, and boy happens to be second in line to the throne. They went to school together; they walked the same St. Andrews streets a few years before I did as a graduate student.

But it is hard, isn't it, to not be taken in by the power of it. The dresses, the palace, the trips to countries all over the world. One day she will be the Queen consort of England; right now, she is a princess. She is beautiful and kind and so warm on camera, so present and genuine.

Hello, she says to a little boy at a charity event. The children have just finished singing; she crouches down in her high heels and reaches out to shake the boy's hand. *Was that you singing just now?*

You sound just like my Georgie. She is a woman who knows how to talk to children. She brings warmth and class wherever she goes, a genteel grace at once genuine and savvy, calculated and fresh.

I have a crush on her, I'll admit it. More than that: for a long time, I wanted so badly to have her life. Her beautiful dresses and her beautiful hair and her smiling, gorgeous children. Everything about the way that she moves through the world feels blessed, magical, extraordinary.

We are taught that *extraordinary* looks and walks and talks a certain way, too. In 2018, when Meghan Markle marries Prince Harry, I watch the royal wedding on my laptop in the early hours of the morning and feel the same old longing ache throughout my limbs. That beautiful dress. The beautiful shoes she wears to the reception. The magical nature of that story.

I wish I had a life like that. I wish I had a body that seemed to fit, as if by magic, into a life like that.

Sure, it isn't everything. Sure, it's only shoes – shoes and a dress and a body that looks a certain way, acts a certain way. The kind of body that can step into a fairy tale, as opposed to the kind of body that does not belong in a fairy tale, or at least not in a fairy tale's happy ending.

Princess.

There is something insidious about the way we conceptualize beauty, about the way we associate gendered values of goodness and purity with what is dainty and pleasing and small. It isn't hard to move from this through to the way we frown upon anything that is larger or unusual or doesn't fit the status quo. It isn't difficult, in other words, to move from the way fairy tales have helped us to conceptualize beauty and goodness through to the way that our ideas of beauty and goodness actually operate in the world.

Perhaps it isn't magic, but for those of us who'll never fit in those shoes no matter how we try, it might as well be.

5

The Little Dumb Foundling:
Hans Christian Andersen's Ugly Little Ducklings

Growing up, 'The Little Mermaid' was my favourite fairy tale. I knew the Disney version first. Rebellious Ariel and her dashing Prince Eric. Scuttle the seagull, Sebastian the crab. Ursula the undulating octopus. Triton the powerful undersea king. Thirty years later, I still know the lyrics to most of the songs in the film.

My Little Mermaid was all red hair and purple seashells, dashing blue-eyed prince, and scheming, tentacled witch. My sister and I wore out our VHS tape so quickly my mother had to buy another; we spent long summer days being mermaids, throwing random objects into the deep end of our swimming pool and diving down to get them. We hummed to each other under the water and said we were *speaking*; we pushed ourselves up to the side of the pool and splashed our legs so that water exploded around us just as it did when Ariel sang the finale of 'Part of Your World.' When we slept, we dreamed of the ocean.

What I didn't realize then — what I wouldn't realize until many years later — was that I had already been a mermaid. Hadn't Ariel's longing for feet been my own dream when I moved around in my wheelchair? When I transitioned to crutches and then worked with a physical therapist to minimize my limp, hadn't I also dreamed of the *jumping* and *dancing* that Ariel sings about, down in her sea cave with Flounder and Sebastian? Hadn't I also wanted the fairy-tale ending that Ariel finds with her prince – someone who loves her and is willing to fight tooth and nail to have her in his life?

I had wanted – still want, if I'm to be perfectly honest – all of those things. Saturated by the Disneyfication of the fable, I also believed I could get it. Weren't happy endings for everyone? If Ariel looked that much more beautiful in her white wedding dress as she stood on that ship, perhaps even more beautiful than she'd been as a mermaid, didn't that mean I could also aim to be that much more beautiful as I stood in my own wedding dress? My own ideas of love and romance always involved a white wedding dress and a handsome prince, and they always involved standing. There were no mermaids, for sure, but there were also no wheelchairs. There were no crutches. There was no limp in that walk down the aisle.

Ariel, of course, gained her legs by magic. I gained my legs by the decidedly less romantic practicalities of orthopaedic surgery, practicalities that left me with a limp that wouldn't go away. Unlike in Ariel's case, the acquisition of my legs was not picture-perfect. And as much as I wanted to believe it to be so, the happy physical ending I thought I had acquired by virtue of surgery and therapy was not, in the end, the kind of happy ending that was talked about in the stories I saw onscreen.

In England, the fairy-tale craze of the eighteenth and nineteenth centuries was spurred by religious confusion and what author and scholar Marina Warner terms *Enlightenment insatiability*. Together, these forces 'spurred divines and scholars to find out what ordinary people believed.' In the face of so much technological and social innovation and advancement, there was a renewed desire to explore and unearth the national past as a way of hearkening back to 'simpler' times, much as the Grimms had been unearthing German history and folk tales and drawing deep on nationalistic nostalgia right at the century's beginning. Thus do we get stories like 'Jack and the Beanstalk,' where a plucky, determined young man of impoverished means outwits the stronger, larger giant, who literally lives on a level apart from the rest of society, surrounded by gold. Other iterations of the 'Jack tales' include Jack Frost (a younger variant of Old Man Winter, alternately drawn as a hero or a trickster) and Jack the Giant Killer (a hero who is said to have slain several giants during King Arthur's reign). The Jack tales also show up in later American history and are a strong part of Appalachian folk history. The main characters in these stories are usually named Jack (or John in certain English versions) and are often initially portrayed as lazy and untrustworthy. Rather than the typical fairy-tale protagonist who is handsome and pure of soul, Jack is not someone you'd initially peg for a hero, but rather a character who is able to triumph thanks to his quick wit and cunning. In this way, he becomes a kind of 'everyman's hero,' speaking to the downtrodden and disenfranchised and subtly imbuing the Jack tales with subversive political concerns. You, too, can defeat the giant – if only you're smart enough.

Hans Christian Andersen, who wrote in Denmark throughout the mid- and late nineteenth century, was, like the tellers of the Jack tales, consumed by stories that spoke to social hierarchy. Born in 1805 to an exceedingly poor family in Odense, Denmark, Andersen lived in poverty for most of his childhood and young adult life. Taken to the theatre by his parents when he was seven, Andersen felt his imagination explode with wonder and seized on the work of reading and writing as the hand that would pull him out of poverty and into a new world. Seven years later, aged fourteen, he left his mother (his father had died in 1816, two years after returning from fighting in the Napoleonic Wars) in Odense and moved to Copenhagen to start that new life.

It wasn't easy. Tall and awkward and continually rebuffed by the theatres to which he would send his plays, Andersen stumbled through the extraordinarily class-conscious Danish society of the time until Jonas Collin, an influential official and patron of the arts, befriended him and paid for Andersen to attend boarding school. Andersen did so for five years, learning how to move and speak and function as a polite member of society.

He was also told repeatedly by his instructors to give up all hope of being a writer – a dictate he promptly ignored after returning to Copenhagen in 1827. He passed the matriculation exam into the University of Copenhagen in 1829 but then decided to embark on a career as a freelance writer. Making a living as such was extraordinarily difficult during the time (sounds familiar), so Collin assisted Andersen once again by helping him secure artist grants from the monarchy.

In the early 1830s, Andersen began to enjoy a modest level of success – a success brought about by his talent as a writer but also his talent for creating a fairy tale of his own life. His autobiographical novel, *The Improvisatore*, was published in 1835, along with some of his first fairy tales, including 'The Tinderbox,' 'The Princess and the Pea,' and 'Thumbelina.' 'The Little Mermaid' and 'The Emperor's New Clothes' joined his fairy-tale collection in 1837. The next year, Andersen began to receive an annual grant from the

King of Denmark, allowing him to enjoy freelance writing as a career for the rest of his life.

Andersen's rise through society, while perhaps not completely meteoric, is nonetheless mirrored by many of the narrative arcs in his fairy tales – the soldier in 'The Tinderbox' claws his way up from poverty to marry the princess and become king; the princess in 'The Princess and the Pea' is, despite her raggedy appearance at first, such a princess on the inside that she feels the presence of the pea through twenty mattresses. The tiny heroine in 'Thumbelina' marries the king of the flower angels at the end of her story and even gains a new name, Maia – one that she is *worthy* of now that she's a queen.

Andersen, in his several autobiographies and his novels, travelogues, and plays, continued to create similar narratives about himself. Over and over again he impressed upon others that he was, as Jack Zipes writes, 'a soldier of fortitude who had the makings of a king, or that he was an oppressed and awkward fowl who would develop into an elegant swan.' He felt ordained for the role of writer in high society in a way that echoes the most well-known fairy-tale trope: individual sets out into the hostile world, ready to overcome and overthrow. And, like the characters who do just this in fairy tales, Andersen pursued happiness *for himself* before looking to change the society in which he lived. In order to obtain what he wanted – fame, status, the ability to create Great Art – he knew he had to game the system rather than change it, and that's exactly what he did.

Which is ironic, really, because Andersen wasn't happy. Plagued by migraines, paranoia, and hypochondria, and unable to net himself a successful marriage despite courting a number of women (while also, it's been documented, harbouring strong feelings for a number of men throughout his life, including Edvard Collin, the son of his patron), Andersen managed to climb to the top of society without ever really feeling like he'd made it – a fairy-tale prince of the nouveau riche, successful and yet forever feeling barred from the rooms in which he longed to play.

Andersen wrote the first-known version of 'The Little Mermaid,' though it was based in no small part on *Undine*, the German fairy-tale novella by Friedrich de la Motte Fouqué wherein a water spirit marries a knight so she can gain a soul. In Andersen's tale, the mermaid, having fallen in love with a human prince whom she rescues from a shipwreck, has her tongue cut out by the sea witch as payment for becoming a human. She must convince the prince to marry her in order to stay human forever; if he marries another, she'll be turned into the foam that crests on the sea. But, though she finds the prince and enchants him with her eyes and her beauty and her dancing – the likes of which have never been seen before at court – she never gets a chance to tell the prince that she was the one who rescued him from the sea in the first place. She has no voice and thus cannot be the same as the woman who rescued the prince. Throughout the latter part of the story, the mermaid is continuously referred to as someone dear to the prince, his 'little dumb foundling,' like a child or sweet sibling who enriches his life; she is infantilized and asexual to him, only a mild supporting character in the unfolding of his life. She gains permission to sleep at his door on a little velvet cushion. Every time she dances or takes a step, the pain in her feet is as if 'she trod on sharp knives':

> She climbed with the prince to the tops of high mountains; and although her tender feet bled so that even her steps

were marked, she only laughed, and followed him till they could see the clouds beneath them looking like a flock of birds travelling to distant lands.

Eventually, the Little Mermaid must watch the prince marry another woman, a princess from a neighbouring kingdom who he thinks is the one who actually did the rescuing. The Little Mermaid, dressed in silk and gold, holds the bride's train at the wedding. That night, in despair, she turns to her sisters, who have conspired with the sea witch to bring her one last chance at life. They hand her a knife and instruct her to murder the prince as he sleeps; only then will she receive her mermaid's tail again and be welcomed back into the sea.

The mermaid, of course, cannot do it. Instead she throws the knife into the sea and jumps to her death from a cliff – one detail that Disney, naturally, cut from its telling.

In the Andersen version, the mermaid doesn't die entirely – instead she becomes a spirit, a 'daughter of the air,' one of hundreds of beautiful, ethereal beings whose job it is to breathe cool air in the wake of pestilence and cure drought; to fly to the ends of the earth and spread the perfume of flowers in order to distribute health amongst the humans. If she is successful in this, after three hundred years, the mermaid will earn herself a human soul after all.

'After three hundred years, thus shall we float into the kingdom of heaven,' said she. 'And we may even get there sooner,' whispered one of her companions. 'Unseen we can enter the houses of men, where there are children, and for every day on which we find a good child, who is the joy of his parents and deserves their love, our time of probation is shortened. The child does not know, when we fly through the room, that we smile with joy at his good conduct, for we can count one year less of our three hundred years. But when we see a naughty or a wicked child, we shed tears of sorrow, and for every tear a day is added to our time of trial!'

Here, we begin to see echoes of the religious dogma that littered the Grimms' *Kinder- und Hausmärchen* – and deep within that, a firm belief in the futility of striving for upward mobility in the face of impermeable social strata. For all his gaming of the system, Andersen seems surprisingly judgmental about who would see earthly reward in their lifetimes and who would not. He is particularly harsh toward his female characters, repeatedly gifting them the kind of pain and afterlife punishments afforded the Little Mermaid.

Perhaps Andersen's most pointed social critique is his fairy tale 'The Emperor's New Clothes,' wherein the vain Emperor is tricked into paying for a dubious set of new 'clothes' by two tailors. The clothes, they tell him, are invisible to anyone unfit for office, tempting the Emperor with what he believes will be the power to ascertain which of his subjects are loyal and which are not. It is a child who finally points out that the Emperor does not have any clothes on and is being paraded around in the nude; only from the innocence of childhood are we able to see and speak past the foolishness of adulthood, with its conventions and social climbing. (No one who sees the tailors preparing the Emperor's new clothes can, in fact, see the fabric; assuming this means they are not fit for office, however, and wanting to hold on to their posts, they buy into the lie and keep assuring the Emperor how beautiful his new clothes are.)

Like the Brothers Grimm, Andersen believed that certain things had been set and ordained by God. He believed he was meant to live a great life as a highly important writer and thinker, and thus was determined to wrestle his way through a society he felt was keeping him from that which he was owed. But though his tales speak against the stratification of society in ways both literal and metaphorical – almost parodically, the Little Mermaid is literally 'brought up' from the sea into a new life on land, and the Emperor is paraded above his people on a litter – they also hold deep within themselves a contradictory truth: some people *aren't meant* to move upward, and might even be punished for doing so. The Little Mermaid is not meant to be on land even though she made her bargain out of love – the pain caused by her transformation would seem to be proof of that. Social upheaval and critique may be all well and good for those who succeed in fighting their way to the top, but for others, it might be accomplished only in the afterlife, and perhaps not even then.

By contrast, some of those who do manage to succeed in Andersen's tales get their earthly – and able-bodied – rewards in the present. In 'The Cripple,' one of Andersen's last-written fairy tales, a wealthy landowner and his wife are kind to a neighbouring family of five children, the oldest of whom is a boy named Hans. At the time of the tale, Hans has been 'weak in the legs' for five years and must lie in bed. 'He was a very clever boy who liked to read, but used his time also for working, so far as one who must always lie in bed could be useful.' Hans is selfless and cheerful, so much so that when the wealthy landowner and his wife, hearing of Hans's growth and maturity, deign to give him some money of his own, he insists that it go straight to his parents. (The beautiful cripple – so useless but so saintly.)

At the beginning of the fairy tale, Hans is given a storybook by the landowners; he uses it to read and travel far away into storybook land. He amuses his parents by reading them the tales; one day, on hearing the loud laugh of Hans's father from the street, the local schoolmaster comes in and befriends Hans. It is this schoolmaster who, sometime later, brings the money from the landowner and his wife to Hans; in response, his parents say, 'Cripple Hans is after all a profit and a blessing.'

Soon after, the lady of the land comes to visit Hans and brings him a songbird in a cage; days later, a neighbourhood cat jumps into Hans's room and threatens the bird. Hans, overcome with love for the bird, miraculously regains the use of his legs, springs from his bed, and saves the day. The landowner and his wife, thrilled with the miracle, send Hans off to the city to be schooled, and his parents keep the old storybook as a way of remembering their boy while he's far away.

(The songbird, interestingly enough, dies of fright during the commotion with the cat.)

'He had recovered his activity again,' Andersen says of the boy, '[for] such things can happen, and it had happened to him.'

Of course we know, looking back on these tales from a century and a half in the future, that these things do not often happen at all. Yet the spirit and the tropes of tales like these persist. The disabled character 'overcomes' his disability through some momentous, miraculous act – or, as in the case of the Little Mermaid, overcomes a variety of disabilities to obtain her heart's true desire through the long work of sacrifice and good deeds.

Pray. Drink more water, drink green tea, do a detox. Push through. Exercise.

The only disability is a bad attitude.

The end goal is the same: the happy ending somehow always involves a body that does exactly what it's supposed to do all of the time. And if you don't manage to get that body, it's somehow entirely your fault. Society has nothing to do with it.

'I was so obsessed with Ariel,' Grace Lapointe tells me, 'that in a 1991 doctor's report – I was two – a doctor listed "provided a synopsis of *The Little Mermaid*" under my intellectual achievements.'

Grace, like me, has cerebral palsy. She is also a writer. She was born the year that *The Little Mermaid* came out in theatres, so she never saw it on the big screen, but the ability to watch and rewatch the film on her VCR was a defining part of her childhood. Interestingly, Ariel's desire to change her body so that she could walk on land was an aspect of the character that Grace always found troubling, even when she was young. In an essay that she wrote for the online magazine *Monstering*, she puts it this way: 'Although I never thought that anything was "wrong" with me, the eerie feeling that something was wrong with Ariel had been unshakable.'

I, too, did not grow up thinking – at least overtly – that something was wrong with me. I had my surgeries, and after the attendant physical therapies was walking again *just like everyone else* – except that I wasn't walking like everyone else, and spent years of energy trying to ignore this.

'Why do you walk so funny?' a young boy once asked me on the school playground.

'I have cerebral palsy,' I said. I could tell that he didn't understand. At the age of eight, even though it had been a part of my history almost from the time I'd begun to have memories, I didn't really understand it either.

'I had an operation at the hospital,' I tried again. 'I had to use a wheelchair for a while.'

'Oh,' he said. Now he got it. 'But you don't have to have a wheelchair anymore.'

'No,' I said. 'I don't.'

Stop talking, is what I wanted to say, but didn't. *I can walk just as well as you.*

Except that I couldn't; except that I didn't. I could walk and run but for the first few years after my surgeries I was told to take it slow. I wasn't allowed to play contact sports – fine by me, since I hated them anyway – but I also wasn't terribly coordinated at the sports that I *could* play, and hated gym class. (In Grade 4 the teacher made us shoot hoops in pairs in competition; my hand-eye coordination was terrible and I hardly ever made a shot. I hated the game so much I started faking injuries just to get out of it. Once, I forged a note from my mother excusing me from gym, only to get sidelined on the bleachers during the play and look up, horrified, to see my mother standing at the gym entrance, asking my teacher why I wasn't playing. She'd come to the school for a PTA meeting.)

Growing up, my legs hurt almost all of the time. The pain was worse in the right leg than the left. Sometimes it was a sharp stab; often it was a dull throb that lasted from morning until night. (*Each time her foot touched the floor, it seemed as if she trod on sharp knives.*) My limp was worse when my legs hurt, so I tried to pretend that there was no pain at all.

I tried to pretend, always, that there was no limp at all. This was survival, although I didn't recognize it as such at the time.

The Little Mermaid was also Sarah Jama's favourite Disney film growing up. For Sarah, the parallels between her own life and Ariel's were all too clear.

'For me,' she tells me, on a bright spring day in April 2019, 'it made so much sense. Ariel wanted to belong to a world she wasn't a part of. And she didn't even fit when she crossed over. [For myself, as a Black disabled woman,] you can't be fully yourself in one space or the other. You're either Black in one community or disabled in another. Ariel was always grappling to belong somewhere else. And she had to physically give something up to be able to do that, and choose to not fully be seen by her family. It was like she belonged literally to two different planets.'

Sarah also has cerebral palsy and uses a wheelchair. In 2016 she was invited by the Liberal government to attend a summit of one hundred youth leaders on disability in Canada. It wasn't until she got there, looking around, that she realized she was the only Black person in the room.

'Justice work is hard when nobody talks about it,' she tells me now. 'How do you create policy when you're in danger of missing entire demographics? As an organizer, you almost have to be hyper-vigilant about how you navigate spaces but also super self-aware. I grew up feeling like I had a split personality. How do you figure out how to navigate both spaces at the same time and be the same person after?'

Like Hans Christian Andersen, Sarah also recognizes the ways in which society has been structured with the upper echelons – in this case, able-bodied people – in mind. But unlike Andersen, she isn't interested in gaming the system. 'Unless there's a financial incentive for society to include disabled people, we're going to continue to be represented in the same time-worn ways.' The witch with her crutch. The blind seer. The sad but saintly boy who lies immobile in his bed.

'The main issue in disability justice is *capital*,' she says. 'There's no way to create a disability-just world or society in the current structure we're in … I see piecemeal attempts to correct these things online without addressing that critical piece – we have to fundamentally redesign society.'

And progress, as we all know, moves like molasses. The Little Mermaid might get her legs and the disabled boy might leap out of bed to save that bird, but what of the other disabled girls and boys who don't get to cross over into this different world? How do we ensure a world that is better for them?

I'm in Grade 3 when a new girl comes to school. She is slim and cool and stylish. I am none of these things. My hair has been slow to grow back these last few years and has come in unevenly – partly curly, partly straight, all of it a mess. For weeks at a time this year I don't brush my hair – I just pull it into a ponytail at the top of my head and forget about it. I have eyebrows like bushy brown caterpillars. I have one shoe that is larger than the other, which isn't really that big a deal but feels like a big deal to me. I feel like everybody can see it.

(Nobody can see it.)

She is very good at gym, the new girl, as good as I am terrible. She is not as good at school as I am, but nobody cares about that. Everyone cares about her clothes – about the Starter jacket she gets before everyone else, about the stylish cut of her jeans, about the way she does her hair. Even those who do not love her instantly – and there are some – watch the way she moves through class. She knows what it means to be *cool* – and also, instinctively, knows what it means to be *not cool*. No one wants to be on the receiving end of that hand, and so they follow her lead almost from the instant she steps onto the playground.

I don't have a chance, really. I am so obviously different in all the wrong ways.

In most fairy tales there is a hero; there is also, often, an antagonist – someone who threatens the protagonist's happiness, someone who throws a wrench into their journey.

The antagonist can be magical – an evil witch, a fairy, a wizard. In many of the tales from the Brothers Grimm, the antagonist is the Devil, hell-bent on bargaining with the protagonist for some part of his soul. Sometimes, as in Aesop and certain other Grimm tales, the antagonist is a faster, wilier animal – the fox is often a villain, as is the wolf or the cat. In many of Andersen's tales, the antagonist is society, personified in both mobs and individuals.

Often, the antagonist is just ordinary. There are weak fathers who let their children be led away in the woods; there are jealous brothers (or sisters) who try to usurp the successes of the favoured (usually youngest) son or daughter. (In most versions of 'Cinderella,' the stepmother is not magical, only rich and cruel.)

In the original version of 'Snow White,' first published by the Brothers Grimm in 1812, there is no examination of the motives of the evil queen – we are made to understand that she is evil purely on the basis of wanting to be the fairest one in the land. With such a dark counterpart, it's that much easier to root for her stepdaughter the princess. *Look how kind she is*, we think. *Look how sweet. Look how unfair her stepmother is – wanting to kill her just because she's beautiful!*

The jealous queen sends her beautiful stepdaughter off into the forest with a huntsman, who confesses the queen's plans to Snow White and then, when she begs him to spare her life, leaves her in the woods. She comes to the cottage of the seven dwarfs and begins to live with them; but the queen, tipped off to Snow White's survival by her relentless magic mirror, disguises herself and makes three attempts on Snow White's life.

First, the queen disguises herself as a peddler and, when the dwarfs are away, comes to Snow White and offers her a bodice as a gift; she laces Snow White so tightly into the bodice that the girl faints, reviving only when the dwarfs return and loosen her ties.

Next, the queen comes to the house as a comb seller and gives Snow White a poisoned comb; the girl faints onto the floor of the cottage and is revived when the dwarfs return and pull the comb from her hair.

Finally, the queen disguises herself as a 'peasant woman' selling apples and enchants one of the apples so that half of it is poisoned. Snow White has been cautioned by the dwarfs not to talk to strangers (sensible, given her recent history) but, charmed by the beauty of the apple and reassured when the woman bites into the safe half, she takes the apple for herself. Upon eating it, Snow White falls down dead.

The dwarfs return and cannot wake her; in despair, they build her a glass coffin and make of her body a shrine in the woods. Eventually a prince comes a-riding and sees the beautiful maiden in the coffin. He's so struck by her beauty that he convinces the dwarfs to let him take the coffin into his castle. The coffin is placed in his room and the prince spends all day looking at it; when he leaves the room and can no longer see it, he becomes sad, so his servants begin to carry the coffin from room to room, following the prince wherever he goes.

One day, a frustrated servant opens the coffin and lifts Snow White out.

'Why must we be plagued with so much work all because of a dead maiden?' he cries. Then he shoves Snow White, dislodging the piece of poisoned apple in her throat, and she wakes up.

The prince, coming into the room to find her alive, is over-joyed. They sit down to dinner and eventually decide to get married. The evil queen is invited to the wedding, and is again tipped off by her mirror that Snow White, having regained her life, is once more the fairest in the land. When the queen comes to the wedding reception, heavy shoes of red-hot iron are fastened to her feet.

'The queen had to put them on and dance in them, and her feet were miserably burned, but she had to keep dancing in them until she danced herself to death.'

And thus, through death and punishment, is balance restored to the universe. The harsh world of the fairy tale once more set to rights. There's no room in a world like this to mourn an evil queen, to question and consider her motives. We're supposed to root for Snow White, and we do, to the point of practically cheering when her evil counterpart is vanquished. Dancing in red-hot iron shoes until your heart gives out seems to me a pretty terrible way to die – to say nothing of the audience of wedding guests who presumably watch it happen – but this is fairy-tale land.

The land, one might say, of just deserts. There might be obstacles and the world might be harsh, but there is order here, of a kind.

Nemesis: from the Greek *nemein*, which means to distribute or allot. Literally, to *give one's due*. Nemesis was the Greek goddess of vengeance, known for meting out justice with equal parts fire and flair. Specifically, her role was to bring to justice those guilty of *hubris*, or arrogance before the gods. Oedipus, whose club foot, as we've seen, has long been thought by scholars to be a symbol of his refusal to bow before the gods, was said to be guilty of hubris.

In English, the term *nemesis* dates from the sixteenth century and was used to refer to retributive justice. The personal sense of the word *nemesis*, referring to someone or something that threatens to defeat you, is a twentieth-century invention.

Another name for Nemesis is Adrasteia, which means *inescapable*.

From the beginning of Grade 3 until the end of Grade 8, when I graduate and move on to secondary school, I have most of my classes with the new girl. Soon she is no longer new but a fixture, the way that the Disney films and the storybooks that line my bookshelves are a fixture in my home. She has red hair, just like my beloved Ariel, but that's where the similarities end. In Grade 3 she calls me Pickle; in Grade 4 she and another girl spend an entire fifteen-minute recess following me around the playground, shouting at the top of their lungs. *Hairy legs! Hairy legs! Amanda has HAIRY LEGS!*

I try to ignore them; I try to pretend they aren't there.

(I am nine years old; I start to shave my legs soon after.)

One day during lunch, the boys sitting behind me start to chant *Aman-DUH! Aman-DUH!* Everybody laughs. I ignore them; I try to pretend they aren't there. It isn't until I get up to go to the bathroom that I realize they've been spitting sunflower seeds into my uneven hair.

In Grade 5, I get breasts before anyone else – the no-longer-new girl laughs at me, and the other girls follow suit. *Hurray, Amanda, you're finally wearing something modern!* one of them says a few days before we finish school for the summer. I'm wearing capris and a long T-shirt; another girl with her looks at me and scoffs. *You call that modern?*

You walk like you've got a pickle stuck up your ass.

I try to ignore them; I try to pretend they aren't there. But there is no order here, no sense of justice. There is no order in what it means to be ten years old and walking with a visible limp; to have unruly hair that covers a network of scars and the bump of a long-dead ventricular peritoneal cyst; to be different and unknown in ways that make no sense to you when you're trying to survive in the schoolyard.

It is not all bad; there is no order to this either. In kindergarten, while I'm away at the hospital, the teacher gets everyone in the class to draw a picture and then laminates them all and binds the pictures into a book. *We Miss You Amanda,* say the words on the front page. There's a black-and-white version of my kindergarten photo on the cover; I have my pre-surgery long hair in the picture, so after I get back from the hospital I don't like to look at it.

In second grade, before the new girl comes, I stand up in front of the class and everyone asks me about my time in hospital. *Did the doctors give her extra brains?* someone asks. *Because Amanda's really smart.*

It might have helped her acquire some extra intelligence, the teacher says. Maybe she is serious, maybe she's just playing along. *But the doctors can't give you extra brains.*

(I am not without friends. I remember sleepovers and birthday parties, long afternoons spent poring over *Teen Beat* magazine. My friends and I like Jonathan Brandis and Jonathan Taylor Thomas. *The Jonathans.*

But when I graduate from Grade 8, I go to the public high school, and everyone else goes to the Catholic one. I never see or speak to any of them again.)

In Grade 5 the red-headed girl and I partner for a school science project. We make a volcano with baking soda and red dye, and I have dinner over at her house a few times, where her mother welcomes me with a warm hug and feeds me chicken breasts and broccoli. The girl teaches me how to tease my bangs into a wave, which is all the rage at that point in time. I stand in her bathroom and look at the two of us in the mirror and think for a moment that perhaps we've turned a corner. I've learned a few things about her – seen her bedroom, the books on her shelves, heard about the TV shows she likes to watch. Maybe things can be different now.

We get a very good grade on the volcano project. I am a very good student. School lets out for the summer. When we come back in the fall, she's no longer talking to me, except to laugh and point once again at my clothes, at my shoulders, at the way that I walk down the hall.

Years after I first saw the Disney film, I read the Hans Christian Anderson version of 'The Little Mermaid.' Now, all these years later, I find myself focused on this image: the mermaid, mute and heartbroken, arcing that one long dive into the sea. She has been mutilated in a number of ways: her tail and tongue taken from her, her ability to connect with others stolen from her as a result of the witch's machinations. She has no hope of convincing the prince in this story, bedazzled as he is by the beauty and charm of his new bride. She is made, by virtue of her disability, *less than* what he might desire.

How should we take this, in this world of modern-day story-telling? Perhaps it's unrealistic to think that a different outcome could have visited this story, especially given the era of its provenance. (The rudimentary beginnings of European sign language were just entering infancy during Andersen's time.)

Still. Surely the Little Mermaid and her prince could have learned sign language, of a kind, or communicated through gestures? Did no one in the palace think to teach the 'little dumb foundling' how to read and write? In the Disney version, Ariel physically signs a contract with Ursula in order to give up her voice. *Couldn't she have written Prince Eric a note?*

But fairy tales have historically been concerned with morals – and historically, *morals* have concerned themselves in a very particular way with the disabled. Hans Christian Andersen's Little Mermaid, as we've seen, is one of those people who might never reach the top of the social ladder, no matter how much they try. (The glimmer of hope at the end of 'The Little Mermaid' seems to me so faint as to not be a glimmer at all.) Disney's Ariel, by contrast, not only manages to regain her voice; her other disability – the immobility afforded by a mermaid's tail on land – is eradicated by her version's happy ending. At the end of the Disney version, Ariel has legs, her voice, *and* her prince. The original mermaid, by contrast, dies with none of those things.

So, suddenly we have two versions of the tale: one in which the disability is vanished and the abled body reigns supreme, and another in which the disability is permanent and leads to grief and suffering. Where is the space for disability as a simple fact of life in a scenario like this? If Ariel couldn't hope to get her prince when she didn't have legs and/or a voice, what hope could a disabled girl like myself have for a life that was free of torment and bullying *unless* she was free of a limp and had all of her faculties intact?

In a study conducted by the Feinberg School of Medicine at Chicago's Northwestern University, forty-four children with cerebral palsy and seven children with other motor disorders (muscular dystrophy, for example, or the effects of stroke) were interviewed about the bullying they experienced at school; 55 per cent of the children reported some form of bullying about their appearance. Being left out of a group and/or being teased and called names were some of the highest reported forms of bullying, with 68 per cent of the respondents noting that this teasing and name-calling dominated their lives at school.

The study authors' hypothesis, at the outset of their research, was that children with the most severe forms of physical disability were the most likely to be targeted for bullying. Instead, as they noted at the study's conclusion, 'we found that children with mild to moderate gross motor impairment seem to be at greater risk for peer and bully victimization than more severely impaired children.'

In November 2018, a fourteen-year-old Nova Scotian boy with cerebral palsy was made to lie face-down in a creek while other teens walked over him, using him as a bridge. The incident was videoed and uploaded to Facebook. After widespread outrage and condemnation, several of the students involved were suspended; the boy received an apology from one of the students, but had trouble returning to school because he felt unsafe.

They're bullies because they don't understand, my parents would say to me, over and over. One day, my father hugged me as I stood at the end of the driveway, sobbing while I waited for the bus. 'The best thing you can do is ignore them. They aren't important. One day, nothing that they say or do to you will matter.'

(He was right. The bullies, the bullying – none of that was important in the end. But I remember everyone's names. I will never forget them.)

I don't want to be like this, I remember thinking all that long, horrid fifth-grade year. *Why do I have to be like this?*

Why can't I be normal, why can't I walk like everyone else? Why is everyone so mean?

Looking back on this now, from almost thirty years in the future, I can see multiple things at once on behalf of that little girl who dreaded getting on the bus every morning. The children I went to school with were not evil – not even my nemesis, persistent antagonist in my life though she was. They were children, responding to a world that had already told them so much about what it meant to move through society in a way that was different. Like the stratified society of Andersen's Copenhagen, their beliefs about what it meant to be different had everything to do with social expectation and success. The schoolyard is a cruel place in the same way that the world is a cruel place – not because of individuals, although that is also true, but because *collectively* we seek to belong, to blend in, to be accepted, and it is easier to shun those who do not fit rather than risk one's own spot in the strata.

'The ideology of ability,' says Tobin Siebers, 'is at its simplest the preference for able-bodiedness. At its most radical, it defines the baseline by which humanness is determined, setting the measure of body and mind that gives or denies human status to individual persons.'

Why can't I be like everyone else? says the woodcutter who longs for a child.

Why can't I be like everyone else? says the lonely queen who wishes for the same thing.

Why can't I be like everyone else? says the Maiden Without Hands, says the Little Mermaid.

Why can't I be like everyone else? says Hans My Hedgehog.

No one is asking the right question. We know that in fairy tales no one has to, because salvation and happiness – even happiness *of a kind* – comes to most of these individuals anyway. Society is not changed, but somehow our heroes come out on top.

Eventually, it seems, everyone in a fairy tale meets one of two fates: they get what they want, which is to be just like everybody else; or they do not get what they want, and they die destitute and alone, a cautionary tale for others who might likewise wish for unattainable things.

But what happens when we ask a different question? What happens when the princess or the childless parent or the half-human boy says instead, *Why* should *I be like everyone else?*

What kinds of stories might we get to tell then?

The skull, writes Dr. Humphreys in my medical notes in 1987, *is of a pleasing shape and symmetry and with a circumference of 52 cm, the measurement is at about the 75th percentile. The ocular movements are full in all directions, except for the left lateral gaze, in which instance the left eye adopts a down and out posture. The fundi* (bottom of the eye) *are clear. There are no evidences of bulbar compromise.*

What does it mean, exactly, for one's skull to have a 'pleasing shape'? Does he mean that it is nice to look at, in contrast to other skulls that aren't? What makes a skull nice to look at?

'Aesthetics,' notes Siebers, 'tracks the sensation that some bodies feel in the presence of other bodies ... The human body is both the subject and object of aesthetic production: the body creates other bodies prized for their ability to change the emotions of their maker.' Essentially, aesthetics – what we find beautiful and pleasing, and the opposite thereof – is about how we as human bodies relate to other bodies. We know and determine what is beautiful – and not beautiful – by placing it in relation to other things around it.

The word *aesthetics* comes to us from the Greek *aisthetikos*, which means 'of sense perception.' In Ancient Greece, the idea of beauty was firmly rooted in balance; Aristotle taught that art and artistic expression were ways of giving life to the essence of something – of unifying both the inner and outer parts of the objects that exist in the world. In his theory of *mimesis*, Aristotle speaks of the perfection of nature as a model for the true and the good; thus is balance and symmetry – that which accurately reflects both the *inside* perfection of something and its outer layer – sought out, while imbalance – that which indicates a flaw or other mark in a perfect design – is frowned upon. While nature is itself always changing, the Aristotelian idea of art and artistic expression is to imitate the world around us but also use mathematics and symmetry to replicate the perfect inherent in the unchanging, *optimum* state of nature.

Thus, beauty epitomizes balance, while that which is aesthetically shocking or displeasing indicates an imbalance that must be corrected. Tellingly, the Ancient Greeks also thought that in order for an object to be beautiful, it had to be useful as well. That which was both beautiful and of use espoused the highest good and the most use to society. If something – or someone – is no longer useful, it cannot be truly beautiful; therefore, treatment of the affected object or individuals involves restoring balance and equilibrium so that utility, in turn, can once more be put in play.

If something is not beautiful, it is no longer of use to society, or at the very least ceases to be regarded in the same favourable way as that which draws from us a positive aesthetic response.

The skull is of a pleasing shape and symmetry.

How might my case have progressed differently, I wonder, if the doctor had determined it was not?

6

'Something Below Humanity':
The Beautiful and the Beastly

The first version of 'Beauty and the Beast,' 'La Belle et la Bête,' was written by the Frenchwoman Gabrielle-Suzanne Barbot de Villeneuve and published in 1740 in her collection *The Young American and Marine Tales.* In de Villeneuve's tale, a wealthy merchant widower loses all of his ships at sea and must learn to live and work, with his twelve children, in a cottage in the forest. His youngest daughter, Beauty, is the most beautiful of his daughters and also the most good-natured: in contrast to her vain and cruel sisters, who do not take kindly to their new lives of poverty, Beauty is determined to make the best of a bad situation. A few years after the merchant's catastrophe, word comes that one of his ships was not lost; setting out in joy to retrieve the goods, the merchant asks his daughters what gifts they would like him to bring home. The older sisters ask for jewels and fine clothes; Beauty, wanting only her father's safe return, asks him to bring her a rose.

The father sets out. On reaching his destination, he discovers that the ship and its assets have been seized to pay his remaining debts, and he is once more destitute; in despair, the merchant turns to go home, then gets lost in a storm and finds himself at the door of a palace. Seeking shelter, he goes in and discovers a house that appears empty, though the candles are lit and the long table in the dining hall is filled with food. Seeing no one to tell him otherwise, the father sits at the table and eats his fill, then makes his way to a bedroom and spends the night.

In the morning, set to go home, the merchant notices a rose garden that sits off to the side of the castle. Thinking of Beauty, he slips in and clips a rose, whereupon he's finally confronted by a 'Beast' who is revealed to be the owner of the castle. Enraged that the merchant has violated his hospitality by trying to steal the rose, the Beast threatens to kill him.

In the de Villeneuve version, the Beast is described as having a trunk like an elephant's and the scales of a fish. He makes great noise throughout the castle with 'the enormous weight of his body, [the] terrible clank of his scales, and an awful roaring.' The merchant is terrified and tries to explain why he wanted the rose; the Beast, somewhat mollified, tells the father that he can leave – but only if one of his daughters comes freely to the castle in his stead.

Despondent, the merchant returns home (laden with chests full of jewels and fine clothes for his children – a parting gift from the Beast, to remind him of what is owed) and tells his daughters what transpired. Beauty, wracked with guilt for asking for the rose in the first place, offers to go to the castle; her sisters, who blame her for the trouble, are glad to see her go.

And so Beauty goes to the castle and stays with the Beast, and though his appearance frightens her, she comes to understand that he means her no violence. At night she is plagued by dreams of a handsome young man who implores her not to trust appearances. 'Judge not by thine eyes,' he says, 'and, above all, abandon me not, but release me from the terrible torment which I endure.' Not understanding the dream, Beauty eventually comes to believe that the young man is being kept captive somewhere in the castle by the Beast. She falls in love with him, but knowing that she can't see him except in her dreams, pines in silence.

The Beast begins to charm her, slowly. Every night at dinner he asks if Beauty will marry him; thinking longingly of the handsome young man from her dreams, she tells him no. Even as she continues to politely refuse the Beast, she develops a friendship with him – but she remains uneasy. 'She should have become accustomed to him,' de Villeneuve writes, 'but he was in love with her, and this love made her apprehensive of some violence.'

(I cannot help but be fascinated by this. *This love made her apprehensive of some violence*. The spectre of a woman afraid of what a suitor might do to her in the face of rejection seems entirely plausible, and ominous precisely because of the way the story has been told and retold through the centuries with this sentiment inside it.)

Some nights, Beauty is visited in her dreams by a mysterious older woman, who exhorts her to remain on her path of friendship with the Beast – and perhaps, even, eventual marriage to him. 'Courage, Beauty; be a model of female generosity; show thyself to be as wise as thou art charming; do not hesitate to sacrifice thy inclination to thy duty.' Who the woman is, however, remains a mystery.

Eventually, though her friendship with the Beast has deepened, Beauty is overcome with homesickness and asks to return for a time to her family. The Beast acquiesces, but warns her that she must return in two months' time or else he will die, presumably of a broken heart. Eager to see her family again, Beauty agrees.

She returns home laden with riches, wishing the unknown prince of her dreams a tearful goodbye. Having expected to never see her again, her family is overjoyed (though her sisters, 'in their hearts, were vexed at beholding her … their jealousy was not extinguished'). Her father and brothers implore her not to go back, but her father begins to reconsider when Beauty tells him of the Beast's repeated offers of marriage.

> '[T]he next time the Beast asks thee if thou wilt marry him, I advise thee not to refuse him. Thou hast admitted to me that he loves thou tenderly; take the proper means to make thy union with him indissoluble. It is much better to have an amiable husband than one whose only recommendation is a handsome person. How many girls are compelled to marry rich brutes, much more brutish than the Beast, who is only one in form, and not in his feelings or actions.'

But Beauty cannot be convinced; in love with the handsome prince who visits her in her dreams, she cannot imagine marrying the Beast. It is only after she has overstayed her two months' time with her family and is visited by a terrible dream that the Beast has died that she realizes she must return. Her father and brothers still try to dissuade her. (Her sisters, who in the interim have lost their own lovers to Beauty's oblivious charm, are the only ones who implore her to go.) But Beauty returns to the castle with the help of a magic ring the Beast had given her.

The castle is almost empty, and Beauty spends a day drifting listlessly about it, waiting for her dinner with the Beast. When dinner comes and the Beast does not appear, Beauty goes in search of him and finds him almost dead in the garden; in sorrow, she runs in search of water and manages to revive him. They return to the castle together, and Beauty retires to her apartment for the night, thinking anew of how kind the Beast has been to her and how much he clearly missed her while she was away. The next evening, at supper, the Beast asks again if she will marry him, and this time, Beauty says yes.

There is a sound outside of artillery, which Beauty understands to be fanfare and celebration. Then there is a magical fireworks display that continues for three hours; when it finishes, both Beauty and the Beast retire for the night to their separate rooms.

That night, Beauty is visited by the old woman in her dreams, who congratulates her for loving the Beast. In the morning, when Beauty awakes, the unknown prince is lying asleep on the couch in her chamber – proof, finally, that the handsome young prince in her dreams was the Beast all along. Soon after this, Beauty and the prince (still asleep) are visited in person by the old woman. Beauty leaves the prince and goes to receive the old woman. She has a female companion with her and is revealed to be the Queen and mother of the Prince; the female companion is a fairy who has orchestrated both the Prince's curse and his release from it, through Beauty.

The Queen, learning of Beauty's comparatively common birth ('What! you are only a merchant's daughter?'), is suddenly displeased, and impresses upon Beauty that she cannot marry the Prince. Beauty, for her part, suddenly agrees.

'When I accepted him,' she says, 'I believed that I was taking pity on something below humanity. I engaged myself to him only with the object of conferring upon him the most signal favour.' (The Prince, having been made temporarily silent by the fairy, says nothing in response to this.) The fairy, displeased herself, reveals the biggest twist of them all – Beauty is, in fact, the Queen's own niece.

Thus mollified by the knowledge of Beauty's true, royal parentage – no matter the incest involved – the Queen blesses the union, and Beauty and the Prince (who, disturbed from sleep by the great noise that the Queen and the fairy have made, has finally awoken and come out to meet the women) are married. The court is dazzled by her beauty and kindness. The story of their courtship is recorded by the Queen and spread, so says the tale, 'throughout the Universe, so that the world at large might never cease to talk of the wonderful adventures of Beauty and the Beast.'

Wonderful adventures, de Villeneuve says. Happily ever after. The end.

When I accepted him, says Beauty, *I believed that I was taking pity on something below humanity.*

For Penny Loker, a Canadian artist and advocate for those with facial differences, the tale of 'Beauty and the Beast' resonates in a number of ways. Penny has hemiofacial microsomia as well as Goldenhar syndrome. The soft tissues and bones in her face did not form properly in utero. She was born missing both the left side of her bottom jaw and her left cheekbone, and her upper jaw was split in two. Her eyelids were almost fused shut, requiring surgeries and repair. As a young child, she knew she looked different but didn't yet grasp how that difference would define the way the world responded to her. That education came as soon as she started school.

'Having grown up with this difference,' she tells me now, her words wry and yet soft, 'my history is long and annoying. For me, it's all I've known; it's been thirty-eight years of non-stop crap, but because it's been this long, I just deal with it.'

There were no friends; there were no slumber parties. The name-calling was a constant part of her life, so much so that she felt she had no choice but to ignore it, hard though that was and continues to be.

Like so many of the people I speak to, Penny found solace in fairy tales – in the blend of familiarity and escape that they offered, in their promise of an eventual happy ending and a world that might get better. 'I was alone and entertained myself for most of my childhood … I always thought that everything would just work out in the end – based on the stories, I'd grow up, have a house, have someone who loved me, and have some kids and be a really awesome mom. But it wasn't until I was older when I started to realize that this wasn't how my life would go. That being shunned by society didn't just get better when you grew up.'

But isn't that what tales like 'Beauty and the Beast' teach the world? The Beast is made *beastly* precisely because his character is so frightening at the start of the story. ('Hold thy tongue, thou foolish talker!' he cries to Beauty's father when his theft of the rose is first discovered. 'I care not for thy flattery, nor for the titles thou bestowest on me. I am not 'my Lord'; I am the Beast; and thou shalt not escape the death thou deservest.') It is only through learning the value of kindness and humility that he is restored to his 'true' form, to his rightful balance of both inner and outer appearance. He is only shunned, in other words, until he learns how to behave, until his *inside makes him beautiful*. And then he is welcomed and feted with all the trappings that a happy ending can muster, while Beauty is praised for her character and goodness, just as she's been praised all the way through the tale.

Yet surely there is nothing innately noble about loving someone who looks different from those around them – especially when, as in the original version of the fairy tale, Beauty comes to realize that the Beast is, in fact, kind and good, and still hesitates to marry him. So why the emphasis on Beauty's noble sacrifice? Why the emphasis, to this day, on the 'nobility' of men and women who marry people in wheelchairs or without limbs or who have facial disfigurements or other outward – and inward – disabilities?

The most signal favour. De Villeneuve's Beauty initially agrees to marry the Beast out of pity. She might no longer be repelled by the Beast, but he is still lower than human to her, something so far beneath her status that marriage is almost inconceivable. Indeed, the repeated urgings from her father about the strength of inner character and heart do nothing. 'How can I determine,' she says, 'to take a husband with whom I can have no sympathy, and whose hideousness is not compensated for by the charms of his conversation? … It is not in my power to endure such a union, and I would rather perish at once than be dying every day of fright, sorrow, disgust, and weariness.'

(It's interesting to me that Beauty also fixates, along with his physical form, on the Beast's perceived 'stupidity' and lack of stimulating conversation as reasons why she's reluctant to accept the proposal, as though there is absolutely nothing left to compensate for his appearance. Reading this for the first time, I couldn't help but think of how society tends to place the disabled within an invisible hierarchy, where the intellectually disabled are often discriminated against even more than physically disabled people. A Beast is one thing, but a *stupid* Beast is something entirely distasteful altogether.)

When Beauty returns to the castle and discovers the Beast almost dead, what shocks her into reviving him and then accepting his offer of marriage isn't love but a sense of obligation and pity. Having realized how good he's been to her, she feels guilty about saying anything else. Far from the teary, whispered *I love you* that she speaks over the Beast's form in the animated (and subsequent live-action) Disney version of the tale, the Beauty in de Villeneuve's tale is hesitant even in her acceptance of the proposal. 'Beauty was silent for a short time, but at last making up her mind, she said to him, "Yes, Beast, I am willing."'

That night, Beauty is visited by the handsome unknown man from her dreams, who rejoices over her upcoming marriage to the Beast. Far from sharing his joy, Beauty is *bitterly annoyed* by his apparent joy at her betrothal to another – it is only after the unknown man reveals himself to be the Prince, the Beast's true form, that she realizes what has transpired. 'How delighted was she … to find that she had done from duty that which she would have done from inclination.'

Tellingly, there is no marring of Beauty's physical appearance to reflect this less-than-kind moment of her own character. Instead we accept it as natural – an understandable gaffe, a sensible reaction to the circumstances.

He was a Beast, someone might say. *Anyone else might have done the same in her position.*

In a later, much-abridged version of the tale modified by governess-turned-author Jeanne-Marie Leprince de Beaumont, the Beast's scales and trunk are removed and he is described as simply 'dreadful,' and there is no quavering on the part of Beauty when she returns to visit her family – only a sudden recognition that she made a mistake in leaving the Beast's castle. 'Why did I refuse to marry him? I should be happier with the monster than my sisters are with their husbands; it is neither wit, nor a fine person, in a husband, that makes a woman happy, but virtue, sweetness of temper, and complaisance, and Beast has all these valuable qualifications.' She returns to the castle and finds the Beast almost dead – here, again, she pours water over his head and he wakes, whereupon she professes her love and agrees to marry him. There is a sudden flash of light and explosion of music, and the Beast disappears, replaced once more by a handsome prince.

In the de Beaumont version, there is no long, drawn-out conclusion with fairies and the reveal of Beauty's royal parentage. Instead, the fairy who cursed the Beast comes and rejoices in his transformation. Beauty's sisters, still vain and jealous, are transformed into statues that guard the entrance to the palace where Beauty and her husband live, condemned to remain in that shape 'until you own your faults, but I am very much afraid that you will always remain statues. Pride, anger, gluttony, and idleness are sometimes conquered, but the conversion of a malicious and envious mind is a kind of miracle.'

De Beaumont was known for the way she inserted moral teachings into her fairy tales. In the same way that the French tales of fairies put the feminine in a story as an agent of change, so too did the arc of 'Beauty and the Beast' aim to speak to a female audience. In this case, we can speculate that the tale was meant primarily for young women who were being passed back and forth in arranged marriages; the you'll-come-to-love-him moral of 'Beauty and the Beast' was more than likely intended as a balm to those who were facing their new lives with some degree of trepidation.

'That the desire for wealth and upward mobility motivates parents to turn their daughters over to beasts,' writes folklore scholar Maria Tatar in the introduction to her collection *Beauty and the Beast: Classic Tales about Animal Brides and Grooms from Around the World*, 'points to the possibility that these tales mirror social practices of an earlier age. Many an arranged marriage must have felt like being tethered to a monster.'

But young women were expected to act and behave a certain way in eighteenth-century France; far from subverting the social structure and calling for reform in the way that her predecessors did, de Beaumont's version of 'Beauty and the Beast' emphasized domesticity and sublimation. Her version of de Villeneuve's tale was included in a collection called *Magasin des Enfans* in 1757, which, Zipes notes, had 'the didactic purpose of demonstrating to little girls how they should behave in different situations.' And thus does the fairy tale begin to make the shift from tool of subversion to tool of the status quo – from stories that seek to give shape to the difference in the world to the stories that urge us all to reach for that same, particular pastel happy ending.

From dark and wild to bright and boring. Where is the triumphant narrative in that, even as the princess walks down the aisle to meet her prince?

In 'The Ugly Duckling,' one of Hans Christian Andersen's best-known fairy tales, originally published in 1844, the duckling born last of all in his brood – his mother sits on this largest egg for days after the rest of her chicks have hatched – is much fuzzier and larger than the others. Dismayed at his appearance, his mother nonetheless swallows her concern and takes the ducklings down to the pond. Seeing her youngest child swimming prettily in the water, she reflects, 'He is my own child, and he is not so very ugly after all if you look at him properly.' Thus it is the duckling's mother who protects him when other animals in the farmyard, dismayed at his appearance, make fun of him and jeer.

'[H]e is not pretty,' she admits, 'but he has a very good disposition, and swims as well or even better than the others.'

But the duckling is mercilessly teased by other farmyard animals, so much so that eventually even his own mother reverses course and says she wishes he had never been born. And so, despondent, the duckling leaves the farm.

His adventures are many and difficult. First he encounters some ducks, and then some wild geese, and he lives with an old woman, her cat, and a hen. When the duckling, far from water, muses about how he would love to swim and drift on a pond, the hen scolds him for his uselessness: 'What an absurd idea … You have nothing else to do, therefore you have foolish fancies. If you could purr or lay eggs, they would pass away.'

(Neither beauty *nor* utility – Aristotle, one might guess, would have no use for the Ugly Duckling either.)

The duckling goes out into the world again. One day he sees a flock of beautiful birds in the sky, which cause him to utter 'a cry so strange that it frightened himself. Could he ever forget those beautiful, happy birds; and when at last they were out of his sight, he dived under the water, and rose again almost beside himself with excitement.'

Winter comes. He is almost frozen in a lake, but is rescued by a peasant who takes him home and warms him up by the fire. The peasant's children want to play with the duckling but the duckling, thinking they'll tease him or hurt him, flees the house in terror. He spends the rest of the winter hiding from the world and skulking through the cold, when at last he finds himself on a moor that has warmed with spring. He tests his wings and finds that they have become big and strong, and flies high into the air, until he spies three of the beautiful birds he remembers from the autumn before, and flies down to them.

'I will fly to those royal birds,' he exclaimed, 'and they will kill me, because I am so ugly, and dare to approach them; but it does not matter: better be killed by them than pecked by the ducks, beaten by the hens, pushed about by the maiden who feeds the poultry, or starved with hunger in the winter.'

But the other birds do nothing of the kind. Instead they recognize the Ugly Duckling for what he truly is – one of them, now grown into a beautiful swan in his own right. Catching a glimpse of his new reflection in the lake, the formerly ugly duckling is astonished at his beauty and also humbled by it. 'Then he felt quite ashamed, and hid his head under his wing; for he did not know what to do, he was so happy, and yet not at all proud.' The tale ends with even the older swans bowing to the younger, handsome swan, and the swan crying aloud in joy. 'Then he rustled his feathers, curved his slender neck, and cried joyfully, from the depths of his heart, "I never dreamed of such happiness as this, while I was an ugly duckling."'

'The Ugly Duckling' is Hans Christian Andersen at his most Hans Christian Andersen. The farmyard is the cruelty of the outside world and its social groups; the trials of the ugly duckling are the trials through which the noble and worthy individual is purified by God. At the end of the fairy tale, the Ugly Duckling, made humble through his trials, is both beautiful and *worthy* of his beauty and good fortune. (One wonders if the Ugly Duckling might have fared so well under Andersen's hand if it had been born female instead.)

'The Ugly Duckling' is used often as a kind of anti-cautionary tale. Far from admonishing or warning others about their behaviour, it is often used to encourage people – particularly young women – that better times are coming. The farmyard that doesn't understand the Ugly Duckling is the world that doesn't yet understand what someone might have to offer; the swans who welcome the Ugly Duckling into their circle at the end are the true community that the duckling has been searching for all along. 'To be born in a duck's nest, in a farmyard, is of no consequence to a bird, if it is hatched from a swan's egg.' What matter the trials and pain of taunts from lower birds when one discovers one has always been a swan?

We can't deny that the swan is objectively beautiful at the end of the story, ugly though he might have been at the story's beginning. In this particular *lack-lack-liquidation* pattern, beauty is the thing that is lacking and is fulfilled in the end, further underscoring the idea that in the stories, beauty comes to those who deserve it.

In reality, though, the Ugly Duckling is never actually ugly – he's only made to feel that way. And he only sees his beauty by recognizing, in turn, how he looks like someone else. The pain and anguish that he endures vanish as soon as the duckling finds himself in a community, reflected in the eyes of those around him.

In 2018 I read Maggie O'Farrell's *I Am, I Am, I Am: Seventeen Brushes With Death*. In a section describing the ongoing effects from a childhood bout with viral encephalitis, I see myself in every word:

I fall or stumble if I don't concentrate. When I ascend or descend stairs, I have to look down at my feet and apply myself to the task of meeting each tread. Don't ever talk to me when I'm climbing stars or negotiating a doorway: these acts require my full attention. I will never play Blind Man's Bluff or surf or wear high-heels or bounce on a trampoline …. I dread book-festival stages with steps – to fall, in front of an audience! …. When I carry babies, especially new ones, on stairs, I do it like my primate ancestors, employing my spare hand as extra ballast.

(I do not carry babies up stairs. I don't think I'll ever trust myself that much.)

It has meant so much for me to find disabled community in unexpected places – to hear a writer I admire detail her difficulties and recognize that those could be my difficulties, too; to see another woman with cerebral palsy talk about her experiences onstage and imagine that that could also be in my future.

But how does a tale like 'The Ugly Duckling' provide solace for someone who recognizes that her own life operates outside of the tidy confines of story? What use is there in reading 'The Ugly Duckling' to a child who has been made to feel ugly as a result of one disability or another, and struggles to find community as a result? The disability, for many of us, does not go away. There is no growing up into an objectively beautiful swan; there is no towering pile of mattresses that will reveal us as the prince or princess that we've always longed to be.

In *Shrek*, the 2001 Dreamworks film that quickly became famous as a cheeky anti–fairy tale, the princess Fiona, turned into an ogre each night due to a fairy's curse, is rescued from the curse at the end of the film by her true love's kiss with Shrek. But to her surprise, Fiona doesn't turn back into the beautiful red-headed princess she was during the day; instead, she remains an ogre.

'I thought I was going to be beautiful,' she says, not understanding. Shrek only takes her hand in reassurance.

'You *are* beautiful,' he says, and surrounded by love, they get their happy ending after all. But it shouldn't escape any of us that Fiona doesn't see herself this way until her new husband tells her so. Ensnared in a firm idea of what it means to be beautiful, the world has told Fiona and countless other princesses like her that in order to succeed in life, to truly get her happy ending, she needs to look a certain way. The fact that she doesn't look that way at the end of the film – and that the audience buys into it – is made possible only by the fact that her husband is also likewise different. They can be different *together*, and thus the world is abdicated of its own responsibility to meet them where they are.

What might have happened to Shrek and Fiona if Fiona had remained a human princess forever? Would the world have been just as eager to see them be in love and build a life? And the Ugly Duckling – what of him? If he hadn't managed to find those swans and see himself reflected in their beauty, would he have found his triumphant way through the world after all? Or would he have been destined to forever see himself as an outcast? Would ogre Shrek and human Fiona have been shunned and whispered at, Fiona the human continually the subject of pitying looks?

Good for you, dear. So brave *of you to be with him when he looks like that.*

What a heartwarming story.

With *Shrek*, and then also with the news stories where a woman in her wedding dress wheels down the aisle in her wheelchair and then triumphantly stands to face her husband; with the story of the woman who stands firmly by her husband after he's disfigured in a fire; with the man who falls in love with a woman who has muscular dystrophy.

It's so good of you to love them. The Beast, Shrek, the Ugly Duckling and eventual swan. The woman in the wheelchair, the man who wears the mask. *I could never do that. And if you do it, then that means I don't have to.*

In 'What the World Gets Wrong About My Quadriplegic Husband and Me,' an essay published on *Catapult* in December 2017, the writer Laura Dorwart recounts being asked, 'How do you bear it?' about her life with her husband, Jason, who is a quadriplegic and uses a wheelchair. 'That must be devastating,' she is told. 'I'm so sorry you have to go through that every day. I can't even imagine.'

Reading these and other lines that she and Jason face on a daily basis, I am struck by how these pitiers unknowingly give voice to the deepest of truths: they *cannot* imagine this kind of life. The inability to imagine a happy ending outside of the confines of the fairy tale is exactly that – a failure of imagination.

'[T]he wheelchair,' she writes, 'that eternal evoker of public feelings – fear, pity, inspiration – functions as the axis of every narrative we can contract, around which everything else turns. Even though you don't want it to, the wheelchair becomes the protagonist, the antagonist, and everything in between.'

The wheelchair, in this case, drives the narrative as much as the perceived ugliness of the Beast and the Ugly Duckling. Hemmed in by expectations of what it means to look different and be different in the world, society is unable to see how happiness might be wrested from a life like this. And so the focus shifts to curing: a world without wheelchairs, a world where beauty follows a predictable and prescribed pattern. We cannot imagine anything else.

'When I lie awake at night,' Dorwart writes, 'the honest-to-god truth is that I don't fantasize about miracle cures and redemption songs. I dream of ramps. Ramps leading up to showers and houses and waterfalls, to haunted hayrides and carriages and job interviews and Capitol Hill … In my dreams … [r]estaurant hostesses and flight attendants are not afraid. Doctors listen. In my dreams, I don't watch him walk. I watch him stop being hurt.'

Some of us don't dream, in other words, of personal transformation as the happy ending.

Instead, we find our points of light in others who might look like us, or share our experiences of tripping up a flight of steps and spilling a full pot of tea. And together we dream about the transformation of the world.

The 'I Am Not Your Villain' campaign launched in the UK in November 2018. A campaign run by Changing Faces, the UK's leading charity for those with visible facial differences, its goal is to raise awareness of the use of scars, disfigurements, and facial differences as 'shorthand' for villainy in television, film, and other kinds of storytelling.

Think Scar from *The Lion King*. The Joker (and Two-Face) from the *Batman* franchise. Think Red Skull in *Captain America*, think Dr. Poison in *Wonder Woman*, think the Evil Queen in *Snow White*, who disguises herself as a hag. Think a whole host of Bond villains (since Daniel Craig took over the character in 2006, three of the four Bond villains have had facial scarring). Think Darth Vader in *Star Wars*. Think Al Pacino as Scarface. Think Freddy Krueger. Richard Harrow in *Boardwalk*

Empire. Wade Wilson in *Deadpool*. Snake Eyes in the *G.I. Joe* franchise. Gregor and Sandor Clegane in *Game of Thrones*. Leatherface in *The Texas Chain Saw Massacre*.

Think Voldemort in the *Harry Potter* books and films, then consider these November 2018 statistics from the *Changing Faces* website:

· Less than a third of children say they would be friends with a child with a visible difference

· Almost half of young people who have a visible difference are bullied at school

· Half of young people say they have witnessed negative behaviour towards a person with a visible difference

Within a month of the launch of the 'I Am Not Your Villain' campaign, the British Film Institute became the first organization to announce that it would no longer fund films that have villains with facial disfigurements or scarring. The decision was welcomed by Changing Faces and many others.

'The film industry has such power to influence the public with its representation of diversity,' said Becky Hewitt, Changing Faces' chief executive, in a November 2018 article in the *Telegraph*, 'and yet films use scars and looking different as a shorthand for villainy all too often.'

'You *can have* a princess with a scar,' says one of the young spokespeople in the 'I Am Not Your Villain' campaign video. 'You can have the person being saved with a birthmark or something, and there's nothing different [about them].'

'When we show people with visible differences as villains rather than heroes,' says another, 'it just kind of sets a stereotype that people who are different can be scary or mean … Growing up, it's very scary because you never see someone like you, someone who might be different, as the hero.'

What kind of different world might we build if our heroes look different, too?

In 'Simple Hans,' another fairy tale from the Brothers Grimm, a king has an only daughter who mysteriously gives birth to a baby boy. No one knows who the father is. Finally, the king orders that the child be taken to the church and given a lemon. The child is to offer the lemon to anyone around him; whoever gets the lemon will be known as the child's father and be married to the princess. The king orders that only high-born people be allowed into the church when this happens.

But a 'little, crooked hunchback' – Simple Hans – who lives in the city and is 'not particularly smart,' hears about the event and makes his way to the castle. He pushes his way to the front of the line and receives the lemon from the baby. The king, mortified, puts Simple Hans, his daughter, and the baby into a barrel and throws it into the sea.

The princess, despairing at her misfortune, lashes out at Simple Hans, who then tells her his secret: some time ago he wished for her to have a child, and he has a secret power that makes whatever he wishes for come true.

'Well, if that's the case,' the princess says, 'wish us something to eat.' Simple Hans obliges; after they have finished eating the potatoes in the barrel, Simple Hans makes three more wishes – for a ship, a magnificent castle, and for himself to be transformed into a beautiful and clever prince. The wishes are granted and the princess takes such a 'great liking' to him that she becomes his wife.

Hans and the princess live together in the castle for some years. After a while, the princess's father goes out hunting and loses his way, then finds their castle. The princess, recognizing him, treats him with great courtesy and he stays in the castle for a while. (The king does not recognize his daughter, thinking she drowned in the barrel years ago.) When the king is ready to go, the princess slips a golden cup into his bags without his noticing and then, after he has left, sends a group of guards to arrest him and bring him back. The king swears that he doesn't know how the cup got into his bags.

'That's why,' the princess says, 'one must beware of declaring someone guilty too rashly.' She reveals herself as the king's lost daughter, and the family rejoices together. Happy endings ensue all around.

Yet once again, the princess learns her lesson only after Simple Hans transforms. It is easier for her to be kind and clear-hearted when confronted with beauty and wit than it is for her to imagine a future with a man such as Simple Hans was at the beginning of the tale. The disabilities of Simple Hans are useful insofar as they exist to teach both the princess and her father a lesson – but once that lesson is learned, there is no need for the disability anymore.

Surely, though, the life of Simple Hans is worth more than someone's teachable moment. What of his secret hopes and dreams? What about all the others out there who live the life of Simple Hans but don't have his wishing power?

What about them?

When she graduated high school, Penny Loker's sister gave her the gift of a manicure and pedicure. She left the salon feeling beautiful for the first time in her life – and then a carload of boys slowed to taunt her as she made her way back home.

'The pretty nails made no difference at all,' she recounted in a 2013 interview with CNN. 'Shamed and humiliated, I realized I was still the same girl that everyone made fun of. I remember that day as one of the worst.'

These years later, she's both pragmatic and honest about what it means to make her way through the world. 'Being stared at, laughed at, and pointed at really doesn't get easier as I get older,' she tells me. 'I think if anything, it's getting harder. I find I'm not forgiving to people's curiosity and do not see myself as someone's teachable moment.' In her YouTube vlog, she is candid and honest about what it means to go through the world understanding that society sees you differently – that the expectations one might have for someone who looks 'normal' are in so many ways different from the expectations that society has for someone who is different in their appearance.

Whenever the facial difference trope pops up in film or on the TV screen – and it pops up all the time – Penny can't help but be frustrated at how these portrayals simplify what is, in reality, a very complex phenomenon. 'Superficially, we're telling young people that who you are as a whole will not be good enough unless you change to be more popular ' – that is, more physically attractive, or even, in the case of the Beast, more *emotionally palatable* – 'and although change can be good … we need to find new ways to share these complex ideas. "Beauty and the Beast" simplifies this to the point where "ugly" is bad and "kind" is pretty – when we all know that that is *not* how the world works.'

'Feelings about evil,' Susan Sontag writes in *Illness as Metaphor*, 'are projected onto a disease. And the disease (so enriched with meanings) is projected onto the world.' As with disease, so with disability. Thus does society tie ideas of weakness to the inability to walk; so does society tie the presence of someone who is non-verbal to the idea of diminished intellectual capacity (lack of speech = lack of communication = lack of capacity to *understand* communication); so do we, in a

Western culture that venerates the idea of beauty and youth, tie the hallmarks of age and loss of beauty or disfigurement to something to be feared, pitied, avoided at all costs so that *we don't catch it*.

Over and above the existence of disabilities both visible and invisible, the *concept* of disability is a thing at once visible and invisible insofar as it affects our conscious ways of seeing. The knowledge of disability makes many able-bodied people uncomfortable, and so they ignore its inherent complications as a way of coping. Ideologically, the world we live in and the stories we've been telling for generations require that everyone be as able-bodied and ideal as possible – as such, the stories we tell around disability are themselves often rigid and unyielding, conforming to the requirements of the social infrastructure that makes up our day-to-day.

In this infrastructure, the fairy-tale princess cannot be in a wheelchair because to be in a wheelchair is to be weak. She cannot have a facial difference because to have a facial difference is to be at best an outcast, and at worst, evil. The fairy-tale prince, likewise, cannot be seen as anything other than strong – physically, as in the case of princes like *The Little Mermaid*'s Eric or *Sleeping Beauty*'s Prince Phillip, or even emotionally and intellectually, as in the case of someone like Aladdin.

Like the social structures that made up the world Hans Christian Andersen railed against, these narratives are so fully entrenched in our society as to be almost indestructible. *Ugly is bad and pretty is good* – easier to keep believing in the trope than to turn the lens back on ourselves and ask why we believe it in the first place.

'Christchurch Mosque Shooter Was Badly Picked on as a Child Because He Was "Chubby" – So He Turned to Violent Video Games, Sparking a Downward Spiral,' ran a headline in

Daily Mail Australia in the days after a 2019 shooting at a New Zealand mosque that killed fifty people.

He was ugly, and picked on, and so he became bad.

'I've lived my whole life looking like this,' Penny says. 'And going on a murder spree to inflict pain and suffering *because* I look like this is not something that has crossed my mind.'

But the stories we've told have said so. The stories we tell *keep* saying so.

The stories make it true.

In the fall of 2013, after my first novel was published and I finished touring, I returned to my hometown and went back to my quiet little life. I had come back to Canada two years before, in 2011, after living in Scotland and pursuing a master's degree. My original plan, and happy ending, had involved emigrating to the UK and living there forever; while I had accepted that I was not going to marry Prince William and live in a castle – deep sigh – I had nonetheless latched on to the idea of building a life overseas, far from the world in which I'd grown up. I loved the romance of Edinburgh, where I'd moved after graduation; I loved the sweep and majesty of the Scottish moors; I loved the loneliness of its isles and the deep, penetrating nature of its wild and unpredictable weather, as much as I bowed under the rain.

What I didn't realize, until I ran out of money and moved home, was that I also loved the freedom that living overseas afforded me from my childhood, and the space and buffer that an international life had given me from my memories of being bullied in school – and also, though I didn't acknowledge it then, from my life as a disabled woman. When I lived far away, I could treat the little Amanda who had grown up in a wheelchair and on crutches and had limped her way through school as an entirely different person, even though that same person was still limping her way through Edinburgh's cobblestoned streets.

Disabled people, went the unspoken thought in my head, did not move overseas. Disabled people did not build lives for themselves far from home. I had done this; therefore I was not disabled.

(Ableism is something we internalize from childhood. It seeps into everything we know. It took me years to acknowledge this, and just as long to understand how it had wound its way into my own life.)

But when I came home, and found myself moving down the same streets that I'd occupied as a child, the sense of moving *backward* was insistent and inescapable. I had thought to overcome the struggles of my childhood by moving away and Accomplishing Things, but somehow that hadn't worked; I had thought that publishing a novel would change things but it didn't. Returning felt like the darkest of defeats. It was hard finding work as a writer, and so for a stretch of years I worked at the very same hospital where I'd received that cast twenty-some-odd years before. First I worked in the blood laboratory, entering bloodwork data into the computer. Then, some months later, I transferred to the Emergency Psychiatry unit, where I checked patients into their rooms and guarded the door, which was locked so that patients couldn't escape.

The Emergency Department, which sat across the hall, was where the girl who had spearheaded making fun of me in elementary school worked as a nurse. Every now and again she would come into the unit and inquire after a patient. She always said hello, and smiled. I said hello and smiled back.

Look, I told myself, *we've both grown up. We've both moved beyond who we were in school.*

But when I walked home from my job at the hospital, I walked home in rage – a slow, creeping rage that manifested in randomly bursting into tears while on the treadmill or in waking up on my days off and deciding to stay inert in bed. As the months slid into fall, and then winter, and then into the spring of 2014, the rage melded with a despair that wound its way around my heart and ribs like the vines that climbed the stones of Sleeping Beauty's castle. I stopped writing. I had an affair; I cried in the bathroom at work and my bathroom at home and during the long, silent walks to and from my workplace.

I slept, I went to work, 2014 became 2015, and winter became spring and then summer again. I woke up every day and wished that I was dead. I thought about running out in front of cars and hoarding my migraine medication and going to sleep one night forever. I got up and went to work because I had no other choice; I told myself I would work until I paid off my student loans, thus freeing my parents from their responsibility, as co-signers, for the debt, and then find a way to disappear.

It would not even be that big a deal, I reasoned. I was living alone by then, and my parents and siblings all had their own lives. I saw my friends when I could but I knew that if I was not around, their lives would more or less proceed exactly as before. I wouldn't write or publish anymore, but as far as I could tell, nothing I had written up to that point had made much of a difference. I had tried to move beyond the world of my childhood and I had failed. Here I was, smack in the middle of my home city, despite having tried for over a decade to stay as far away from it as I could. Nothing I could write would ever move beyond that, beyond these borders. What did it matter if I died and was no longer writing?

It didn't, I told myself. It didn't matter at all.

7

The Desolate Land

In the Brothers Grimm version of 'Rapunzel,' Rapunzel is born to a woman who, consumed by pregnancy cravings, convinces her husband to sneak into the yard of the witch who lives behind their house and steal some of the rapunzel that grows in her garden. The witch catches the husband in the act and demands their first-born child as payment; when the child is born, the witch whisks her away. She grows into 'the most beautiful child under the sun.' When Rapunzel turns twelve, the witch brings her to a tower, where she is imprisoned for the next few years and grows into a young woman.

One day, a prince comes by the tower and hears Rapunzel singing. Bewitched by her mysterious, unseen voice, the prince returns day and night to her tower until he witnesses a visit from the witch, Mother Gothel, who climbs up into the tower on a ladder of hair after uttering the words *Rapunzel, Rapunzel, let down your hair*. After the witch leaves, the prince repeats her words and climbs into the tower. After getting over her initial shock, Rapunzel is charmed by the prince and allows him to make regular visits into her tower.

(In the seventh edition of the tale, published in the 1857 collection, Rapunzel tells the prince to come back each time with a skein of silk, which she will weave into a ladder. It is endlessly interesting to me that the prince doesn't come back with his *own* rope, ready to rescue the maiden – nor does he alert his kingdom to her captivity and come charging to the tower with army at hand. She is better in the tower – contained, special. As long as she's in the tower, *she exists just for him.*)

Sometime after this, the witch discovers the deception. (In the version of the tale published in 1812, Rapunzel becomes pregnant and carelessly asks the witch why her clothes have become so tight; in the later versions of the tale as edited by Wilhelm Grimm, the deception is uncovered when Rapunzel guilelessly asks the witch why she is so much heavier to pull up into the tower than the prince.) In a rage, the witch shears off Rapunzel's hair and removes her from the tower, taking her 'to a desolate land' where she must live 'in misery and grief.' The witch then returns to the tower and hangs Rapunzel's braids out of the window as enticement to the prince. It works, and when the prince climbs the hair and discovers the witch in the tower, she warns him that he will never see Rapunzel again.

In despair, the prince jumps from the tower. He survives, but falls into a bush of thorns, which pierce his eyes and make him blind.

In Jack Zipes's 2014 translation of the first edition of the Brothers Grimm tale, the prince 'strayed about in the forest, ate nothing but roots and berries, and did nothing but mourn and weep about the loss of his dearest wife. There he wandered for many years in misery.'

('Dearest *wife*': interestingly, for all of Wilhelm Grimm's religious editing, there is no note in subsequent editions about when and how Rapunzel and the prince actually get married.)

Eventually, he made his way to the desolate land where Rapunzel was leading a wretched existence with the twins, a boy and a girl, to whom she had given birth. When he heard a voice that he thought sounded familiar, he went straight toward it, and when he reached her, Rapunzel recognized him. She embraced him and wept, and as two of her tears dropped on his eyes they became clear, and he could see again. Then he escorted her back to his kingdom, where he was received with joy, and they lived happily and contentedly for a long time thereafter.

I am intrigued by this *desolate land*. I have been there. I know its dips and hollows, the absence of its trees. What did Rapunzel do in the years when she walked its stubbled hills? Did she wake up every morning and wish her life away, like I did? Did she feed her twins and wish hard for a storm or a sickness to come and take them away? And the prince – what did he wish for as he stumbled around eating those roots and berries? Did he think longingly of the life he used to have and the dreams he might have harboured with the golden-haired girl in the tower? Did he curse her? Did he scream out, *This isn't fair?*

In the fairy-tale world, time passes in the blink of an eye. It can also last forever, the way one hundred years spans whole generations. (In the Charles Perrault version of 'Sleeping Beauty,' the princess awakens after one hundred years into a world where fashion has marched onward and left her blatantly behind the times. The prince refrains 'from telling her that her clothes, with the straight collar which she wore, were like those to which his grandmother had been accustomed.')

In the summer of 2015, the deepest part of my depression, time felt eternal and also instantaneous – each moment crystalline and electric while also somehow dulled, exactly the same as the moment that had come before it and the moment that would come after. There are technical terms for this brain fog, but it still feels right to me to call it magic – never before have I felt so imprisoned by something that wasn't a prison, something that was merely my own life. It made sense to think of it as wizardry, a kind of spell that had come down into my life the way that Rapunzel and her twins had been brought down into despair through the hands of that witch.

In the sixteenth century, when Giambattista Basile wrote 'Sun, Moon, and Talia,' the first version of 'Sleeping Beauty' that we know, depression was an unknown, something as mystifying and magical as the stars in outer space. In Basile's tale, Talia, the daughter of a nobleman who lives on a country estate, pricks her finger on a splinter of flax and falls into an unwakeable sleep. Her father lays her out on a bier in the main hall and abandons the castle. Some years later, she is discovered by the king, who has gone on a hunting trip and comes across the castle in the woods. She is definitely asleep when he first sees her and 'gathers the first fruits of love'; she is awakened only by the birth of her twins some nine months later, who are helped to her breast by two benevolent fairies who have come to attend the birth.

There is nothing in this original tale that speaks to the heinous nature of this act – the fact that the king is so overcome with lust that he gathers the sleeping maiden into his arms and rapes her while she's unconscious. Then he leaves the castle and forgets about her ('[F]or a time [he] thought no more about this incident'), only to remember her some months later and return to find her with her babies. Presumably, not knowing about the birth, the king is returning to have sex with Talia again. He spares no thought for her in this matter, only for his own needs. Like the character Stefan in the Disney film *Maleficent* who would come along centuries later, the king is concerned first and foremost with his own pleasure and gratification.

It is fascinating to me – in the most terrible of ways – that the violation of each character plays out in a very specific manner. Both Talia and Maleficent are drugged in their stories – one by magic, one through a medicinal potion – and have something taken from them in the drugging. Talia's (presumed) virginity is stolen from her; Maleficent's wings are taken away. Talia is raped because she is sleeping and the king feels no need to obtain her consent, while Maleficent is violated because Stefan wants to bring her wings back as a trophy. In both cases, the women are seen as something *other*, and their respective elements of self are seen as prizes for someone else to take.

In particular, I am struck by the fact – as Errol Kerr noted in Chapter Four – that the removal of Maleficent's specific mode of mobility amounts to a kind of violation with which many disabled people can identify. In removing her wings, Stefan is taking away the very thing that makes Maleficent *Maleficent* – she does not move like other creatures, but she is now forced to move like them as a result of someone else's machinations. She is seen as other, as less than human, and thus does Stefan justify the removal of her wings. And while we understand the terrible nature of her wings' removal in the film, I don't think many people understand that the removal of mobility aids, whether through cultural pressure or otherwise, that many disabled people face on a daily basis amounts to the same thing. A wheelchair, for example – like Maleficent's wings – can be an integral part of a disabled person's day-to-day. It shapes how they navigate and see the world. To encourage (force) them to want to walk instead is to remove a very specific part of who they are.

And yet we have not, traditionally, conceived of mobility and other disability aids this way, in much the same way that we, as a society, have not frowned upon the seedier (indeed, downright horrifying) elements of the traditional versions of our most beloved fairy tales. Instead, society views the removal of mobility aids and the 'reinstatement' of traditional ability as the happy ending, in much the same way that the initial English translation of 'Sun, Moon, and Talia' ends on two lines of poetry that position the rape of the maiden as entirely worthwhile in the end: *'Lucky people, so 'tis said / Are blessed by fortune whilst in bed.'*

Rape notwithstanding, Talia is probably not depressed in this story; neither is it likely that she had Kleine-Levin syndrome, a condition where individuals experience prolonged episodes of sleep. Basile was working with magic, not with disease. But the fact that Kleine-Levin is also known colloquially as 'Sleeping Beauty syndrome' speaks to how intertwined our experiences of story and disability are – once upon a time, we used story to explain the disabilities that we didn't know, and now we use story to explain the disabilities that we *do* understand, situating them in the world using cultural touchstones that explain to us what medical terminology cannot. A person in the Western world might not know what narcolepsy means, but there's a high probability that the story of Rip Van Winkle has made itself known to them in some way over the years – so too with Sleeping Beauty, and Cinderella, and Rapunzel, and all of these stories that weave so thickly through us as we make our ways through the world.

For Kelly Aiello, the construction of mental illness in fairy tales is synonymous with negative representation.

'A lot of the villains in fairy tales would fall under the DSM-5 as having a personality disorder,' she tells me. The DSM, or *Diagnostic and Statistical Manual of Mental Disorders*, is put out by the American Psychiatric Association to classify mental disorders (the fifth edition was published in 2013). 'The overarching idea that personality disorders would thus be characterized as evil is problematic to start with.'

Kelly is a Toronto-based writer and editor. In 2018, she co-founded *Alt-Minds*, an online and print journal that seeks to highlight and promote fiction, non-fiction, and poetry written by those who have experienced challenges with their mental health. The way we tell stories – and how we use these stories to stigmatize and isolate the experience of mental illness in particular – is inextricably linked, for her, to the way we perceive illness in the world.

'If you look up the criteria of any personality disorder,' she says, 'they pretty much pathologize any behaviour which is not considered socially acceptable.'

In a 2007 study on gender bias in diagnostic criteria for the DSM, study authors J. Serrita Jane, Thomas F. Oltmanns, Susan C. South, and Eric Turkheimer note that established personality disorder criteria 'assume unfairly that stereotypical female characteristics are pathological.' In much the same way, certain negative characteristics of fairy-tale villains often fall within a gender bias: the evil stepmother is the stereotypical narcissist, obsessed with beauty and youth, while male villains (and even protagonists, to a degree – Jack, after all, emerges triumphant after successfully tricking the giant) are often characterized as tricksters and swindlers, a kind of deception that falls under the realm of anti-social personality disorder. In both instances, the villains want power, but that power is conceptualized in very specific gendered ways; the stepmothers in both 'Snow White' and 'Cinderella' want the reward that comes with expert wielding of beauty and sexual agency; villains like Rumpelstiltskin and the Devil in the Grimms' depictions want human life and its earthly counterpart, wealth and riches.

Once again, we come up against the fact that the fairy tale is firmly situated in culture, continuously shaped by the society in which it thrives. In a world where the only powers granted to a woman have historically been beauty and sexual currency, it makes sense to endow a female character with that power; so too does it make sense to endow a male character with those characteristics that might help him achieve the traditional idea of male success.

But it's also true that these stories, in turn, shape the society in which they exist. If the stories that you tell repeatedly associate female agency and power with a queen's greed and narcissism, it's not difficult to begin to see female agency itself as a questionable thing – both when you live in early modern societies steeped in folk tale and fairy mythology, and also when you live in a modern Western world likewise steeped in stories about what it means to be a girl. While I was researching this book, one Google search for 'fairy tales and mental illness' brought me a treasure trove of information; the top three hits are all variations on '15 Disney Princesses Who Actually Suffered from a Mental Health Disorder.'

There is no mention of Disney princes and whether or not they might also be struggling, because we do not really associate the prince with any kind of struggle.

Bitches be crazy, on the other hand, is a refrain that everyone knows.

Let's return, for a moment, to the changeling. We often think of changelings as babies – of a baby being snatched out of its cradle and replaced with another child – but in earlier times it wasn't unheard of for the changeling phenomenon to happen later in life.

In the case of Bridget Cleary, the Irishwoman who was killed by her husband in 1895, the 'fairy defence' used by Michael Cleary stated that Bridget herself had been replaced by a changeling, a fairy that Michael had killed with the intent of having his wife returned to him unharmed. Concerned that she was exhibiting strange behaviour after a short period of illness, Michael had confided in a friend of his, John Dunne, a local man known to be a *seanchaí*, a storyteller versed in fairy mythology. Dunne suggested that Michael go to Denis Ganey, a local 'fairy doctor,' who prescribed a concoction of herbs for Bridget to drink; when it took three people to hold Bridget down and force the bitter liquid into her mouth, Michael was further convinced of her changeling status. His repeated exhortations for his wife to state her name – *I am Bridget Boland, wife of Michael Cleary, in the name of God* – were not answered to his satisfaction. His suspicions, flamed by Dunne and confirmed by Ganey, culminated in Michael setting Bridget ablaze in their house a few days later while her family was present; he then disposed of her badly burned body and told her family not to tell the authorities.

Two days later – days in which Michael Cleary repeatedly rode his horse around a nearby 'fairy hill,' waiting for his wife to be returned to him – authorities found Bridget Cleary's body buried in a boggy area close to the Cleary house. Michael and several others – including four of Bridget's cousins, as well as John Dunne – were arrested and brought to trial.

The case received widespread attention in the Irish media, with many using the case as an opportunity to warn against the pervasiveness of fairy myths. 'If these dreadful cases are not indicative of any general condition of intensive superstitious depravity in Ireland,' wrote Michael McCarthy in the 1901 book *Five Years in Ireland*, 'but are more or less isolated cases, then our note of condemnation should be all the more distinct and unequivocal.'

Bridget Cleary was uncommonly independent for her time. She was known as an attractive and industrious young woman whose work as a milliner and egg-seller contributed to her household; rumours of marital trouble between the Clearys had existed for some time (there were whispers of a lover, and during her illness, she confided to an aunt that she thought her husband was 'making a fairy of her' and had wanted to do so for months). Perhaps she was gaining strength in her independence; perhaps she was irritable and out of sorts after a period of illness and thus seemed not herself. Her husband reportedly insisted that she seemed 'too fine' to be his wife, as well as two inches taller than the woman he had married.

Subsequent studies of the case have advanced the theory that Michael Cleary himself had suffered some kind of psychotic break due to the stress of his wife's illness. Capgras syndrome – a disorder wherein someone believes that a person they know has been replaced by an imposter – has been advanced as a possible explanation for Michael's behaviour. Tellingly, Capgras syndrome is heavily influenced by personal context – like the folk and fairy tales we've told ourselves for centuries, it is an illness that derives its shape and character from other stories.

The stories, once again, make it true.

In Grade 7, I spend one week of school home sick with the flu. When I return, there are whispers and sidelong glances at me in class; there are snickered laughs behind people's hands and exaggerated eye rolls during lunch when people think I'm not looking.

'Sheila says you called her a bitch,' someone tells me. Perplexed, I go to Sheila and try to set the record straight, but she does not listen.

'You *did* call me that,' she insists as we stand in line at the doors after recess, waiting to go back into school. I can't get anything else out of her.

I don't know where her certainty has come from, but later that night, over dinner, my sister tells me that people in her class are talking about how I had written things about my classmates down in my journal at school. One day at lunch hour while I was home sick, my classmates had gone into my desk and taken out my journal, then read it out loud for all to hear.

My parents call the teacher, who promises he'll deal with it. Several days later, he cancels recess and tells the whole class they are staying in, and tells them why.

'We're going to get to the bottom of this,' he says. 'I want to know who went into Amanda's desk and took out that journal, and I want to know who did it now.'

No one confesses, but no one disavows it either. I want to be somewhere else so badly that it hurts.

Finally, someone speaks. 'Well,' the student says, 'even if we did – how come she gets to write things like that about other people anyway?'

'That's true,' my teacher says. 'Amanda shouldn't have written anything about her classmates in her journal.'

It is hard to breathe; it is hard to keep my eyes open and focused. It is hard to do anything else other than scream, but I do. I sit at my desk and stare at the floor, my classmates fuming in silence around me.

'I will be talking to Amanda about that,' the teacher says. 'She will be disciplined accordingly.'

Twenty-five years later, my memory of what was actually in that journal is hazy, and I no longer have the journal to verify. I don't think I called anyone a bitch – it was a Catholic school, and I took that very seriously. Swearing was *not allowed*, even in one's private papers. Besides, our teachers read the journals as a way of ensuring that we completed assignments. If I had called someone out in the journal in that way, you can bet that my teacher would have called me out on it long before that day in class.

I do remember writing that the world was unfair. *Why do some people get to have everything*, I asked the smooth blue lines of my notebook, *and others nothing at all? Why do some people get to be popular and pretty while others are ignored? It isn't FAIR.*

It isn't fair. It isn't fair.

It wasn't fair then and it isn't fair now. It isn't fair when the disabled body is overlooked and forgotten because the princess or the prince is the one whose story everyone wants to follow; it isn't fair when the person with the visible difference gets cast as the villain in the story because that's the only place where anyone can imagine they might fit. It isn't fair when the institutional power of the able-bodied world gangs up on the disabled body the way those classmates sat around me in that room so long ago; when that power says, *Why is this person speaking out*, and the rest of the world agrees with the question and says, *They shouldn't be saying these things at all.*

That day in class, I learned it was better to refrain from speaking out, even secretly. To pretend that you belonged even if the world didn't make you feel that way. There was power in assimilating. It was a power that had little to do with strength and everything to do with survival – in order to make your way through the world, it was best to keep your head down, to avoid questioning the status quo, even if – especially if – that status quo had very specific instructions about what it meant to move through the world at all.

It was best, I learned, to pretend to be able-bodied – to stop questioning *why* the world was unfair and instead act as though it was fair, even if I didn't always feel it. Asking too many questions about who got what and who did what to whom was trouble I wasn't equipped to face.

Why can't I be like everybody else? I said to myself when I went home that night those years ago. Just like Hans My Hedgehog, just like the Little Mermaid.

There was no answer to that question, not then. Instead there was only a solution: if I couldn't be like everyone else, I could at least pretend to be that way. *Fake it till you make it*, as they say. If I got good at pretending, maybe I could fool the whole world as much as I fooled myself.

In the darkest days of my depression, I lay in bed on my days off work and watched hour after hour of television. I was particularly enamoured with *Sense8*, a series created by Lana and Lilly Wachowski and J. Michael Straczynski that followed a group of eight individuals who wake up one day to find themselves psychically connected. It was not a show based on a fairy tale, but the structure of it felt that way – here were people making their way through a hostile world, the connectedness of their minds taking the place of traditional magic. I watched each episode and wished desperately for the sudden power afforded these characters – the ability to step into a world wholly new, the community that came to them in the wake of this sudden, life-altering difference. The eight individuals in the series were at once singular and yet firmly entrenched in similar experience – the arc of the show was about understanding their community as much as it was about the discovery of their shared collective power.

My life, by contrast, felt like it was drifting further and further from any kind of community at all. I was lost in the forest. I stopped going out with friends. I stopped seeing my family. When my parents, worried, asked me if I was okay, I brushed them off and said that I was fine.

It's okay, I told them. *It's just a little situational depression.* My part-time job at the hospital was not making me enough money, and I constantly worried about the need to find more work; I was paying back student loans; I was trying not to stare the gaping reality of life back in my home city in the face. Life felt insurmountably busy and yet also impossibly small. I'd had big dreams for myself of an international life, and they were gone now; escaping into story was the only way I got through the day.

And yet I told myself every day that I was fine – just a little sad, just a little underwhelmed by life. My life was not terrible, a fact that I reminded myself of every morning. Didn't I have a roof over my head and food in the fridge? Wasn't this objectively better even than living in Scotland, where I'd been so poor it had been a struggle to make sure I could eat?

You're okay. You're fine. You can do this.

Nothing's wrong.

I was *fake-it-till-you-make-it* deep in denial.

In the summer of 2015, when my depression was at its worst, a nurse that I worked with in the Emergency Psychiatry unit took me aside and told me that I needed to get help.

'You're not yourself,' she said. 'And you haven't been yourself for a long time.'

For some reason, the fact that she could tell something was wrong was what hurt the most. Hadn't I been faking it, and faking it well? No one knew. My parents and a few of my friends had been asking if I was okay, but hadn't I fooled them? Hadn't I been pretending all along – first that I walked just like everyone else, and then also that I was happy?

I am myself, I wanted to tell that nurse. At the same time I wanted to cry on her shoulder. *I am Amanda Leduc, in the name of God.*

And yet no one believed me, because everyone could see.

Two hundred years ago, might my family and friends have looked at me, haggard and grey in my depression, and thought I'd been replaced by a changeling?

Would a mother, thick in the throes of postpartum depression, perhaps have looked at her baby and thought it didn't belong to her, wasn't her own, and blamed the fairies instead? Would her husband and family, faced with the listlessness and unpredictability of the new mother in the house, have suspected a changeling swap of the adult woman, too?

In a 2014 dissertation on Scottish folklore and history, scholar Mariah Hudec notes that the changeling myth was exacerbated by additional folkloric beliefs and traditions around childbirth – namely, the practice of the new mother 'lying-in' after the birth, a period of time of up to one month where a new mother was isolated in the house and could only be visited by women. Given the volatile nature of that period of time, it's likely that the prolonged isolation brought on by lying-in heightened traditional symptoms of what we now know as postpartum depression, furthering distance between mother and child and hampering the bonding process, which would no doubt have had physical effects on an infant. 'Feelings of incompetence or uncertainty related to childcare could thus have become a self-perpetuating reality for early modern mothers,' Hudec writes. 'Children who developed a poor relationship with their parent could thus begin to experience some of the physical effects that were part of the changeling motif.'

Later, Hudec cites a specific case – the trial of Isobel Haldane, who was tried for witchcraft in 1623. The case, laid out in *Ancient Criminal Trials of Scotland*, noted the peculiar physical effects of lack of maternal-child bonding: 'Isobel Haldane was visited by a mother for help with "hir bairne that wes ane scharge."' Writes Hudec, 'The Dictionary of the Scots Language defines the word *sharg* as "shrivelled from infirmity; puny. A sickly child." Thus we have a physical description of a 'changeling' similar to those provided by [Scottish scholar Lewis] Spence and the [Stith] Thompson motif-index of folk-literature.' And so does story lead to action lead back to story again, all the way to the Aarne-Thompson-Uther Index.

It's interesting to note here that the ultimate fallout from changeling stories is the dehumanization of the infant or affected adult. Bridget Cleary was killed by her husband presumably because he no longer believed she was human – the same reasoning often applied to the sickly or disabled child left outside to die in the snow. If the child is not human, there cannot be culpability on the part of the person who leaves the child out to die.

If the disabled and ill body is seen as *less than human*, then there cannot be as much of an outcry when the disabled life is also, likewise, seen as less. When Canadian farmer Robert

Latimer killed his daughter Tracy in October 1993, his reasoning was that her life, filled with pain as it was, did not seem worth living. Tracy had a severe case of cerebral palsy with significant developmental and physical disabilities. 'With the combination of a feeding tube, rods in her back, the leg cut and flopping around and bedsores,' he was quoted as saying in a 1997 article in the *New York Times*, 'how can people say she was a happy little girl?'

In modern times, the folk-tale origins of the changeling transmogrify into the cultural beliefs that persist around prominent psychological disorders – conditions that often, quite literally, make an individual into a different person. Schizophrenia, for example, is heavily influenced by culture: delusions in patients treated in the 1970s and 1980s often centred on Russian spies, while patients who came into the Emergency Psychiatry ward where I worked in the early 2010s often talked of ISIS sending them messages through the computer. And while we no longer put babies out in the snow, the isolation of those who are deemed different is still fairly common practice. Those with mental illnesses are shunned both culturally and socially – avoided the same way the world avoids many of those with physical disabilities. While much has been done in recent years to counter the stigma surrounding mental illness, if we are going to harness the true power of revisioning our stories and beliefs about mental health and mental illness, we need structural and political change.

Bell Let's Talk, an annual campaign run by the Canadian multimedia giant Bell Media, centres on Bell Let's Talk Day, a given day in January when conversations around mental health are bolstered and promoted on social media. Each tweet and retweet using the hashtag #BellLetsTalk is tracked by Bell and allotted a donation by the company – at the end of the day, the total amount of money garnered through social media activity is donated to mental health initiatives across the country. Between the start of the initiative in 2010 and 2018, Bell Let's Talk raised $86.5 million.

The campaign has been credited with playing a role in the wider acceptance of discussions about mental health in society, specifically in the workplace. It has been criticized, however, for the part it has played in the corporatization of mental health – the campaign raises money for mental health causes but also affords Bell free publicity in the form of millions of social media interactions and discussions both before, during, and after the January campaign.

More importantly, the campaign seems especially suspect in light of testimonials from previous Bell Media employees, who argue that they were let go from their jobs after disclosing mental health concerns. In a 2017 investigation by CBC's *Go Public*, Jessica Belliveau, who worked for a Bell call centre in Moncton, New Brunswick, disclosed that she quit her job working for a Bell Media subsidiary due to stress caused by the need to constantly meet her targets. In November of 2017, former Bell call centre employee Andrea Rizzo filed a complaint with the Canadian Human Rights Commission, claiming discrimination because of a disability. She had carpal tunnel syndrome, but although she'd had two doctors recommend she receive workplace accommodation in the form of reduced sales targets, her managers had put her sales targets back up to their original level in December 2016.

Another problem with Bell's campaign is that it absolves the public and the government of the responsibility for looking at the systemic issues that make the charities that the campaign supports necessary in the first place. Raising awareness about mental health and demolishing the stigma around mental illness is a good and worthy aim. But raising awareness is only part of the problem – framing the disabled as grateful recipients of a charity's benevolence perpetuates the idea that the disabled are worthy only insofar as they make good objects of pity.

And if a disabled person is not a *good* object of pity – if a mentally unwell individual is not a *good* example of the struggles one can have with mental illness – then the pity shifts to belief that said individual doesn't deserve whatever said charity might purport to help them achieve.

If you are not a good spokesperson for a charity supporting those with facial differences, for example – *if you don't do what we tell you* – then perhaps you are not a good beneficiary of said charity.

If you are not a good employee, if your mental health concerns are not *palatable*, then perhaps you don't deserve help and do deserve to get fired.

If you are not a pretty princess, or a likeable narrator out in the world, then odds are you're not going to get your happy ending, because you don't deserve it.

When I think back to that time now, that stretch of years from 2013 to early 2016, the image that comes most strongly to mind is that of a zipper. I wanted to grasp a zipper at the top of my head and pull it down so that I could step out of my skin as one might move out of a dress – to step out of my being and my life and move quietly, invisibly, into someone else's, or into no life at all. But how do you escape sadness when it permeates every corner of your day? Where do you go when even your dreams are filled with worry and grief, when your mind is exactly the thing you can't escape? How do you come back from a way of seeing where even the gifts of your own life don't seem like gifts anymore?

In an interview about her 2018 book *Happy Never After*, Scottish author and journalist Jill Stark talks about what she calls 'the fairy-tale filter' — that structure of the happy ending that so many of us superimpose onto our lives. In her case, the fairy-tale filter came after the publication of her memoir, *High Sobriety: My Year Without Booze*, which was published to worldwide acclaim in 2013. Faced with the success of her book, Stark couldn't understand why her depression and anxiety were mushrooming out of control — hadn't she achieved the dream? When passersby and readers commented on her success, why did she find it so hard to smile and nod in agreement?

> We look at things ... through a fairy-tale filter — whether through advertising or through Hollywood movies — we're always plodding along to the destination, and then we get there. So we plan for the wedding, not the marriage; we plan for the birth, not the baby ... and you get to the end of the wedding and it's like, *well now what? Nothing's changed!*

Once upon a time, I watched Ariel swim in the ocean as her Disney mermaid self and imagined my life as a mermaid. And yet the happy ending that was hers ended on a wedding boat, arm-in-arm with her prince. There was movement all through her story right up until the ending, when everything stopped.

Now what? I'd been asking myself since coming back from Scotland. I'd had a life with movement and now it felt as though everything had come to a standstill. *Now what happens?*

What happened next, thanks to the recommendations of that nurse who told me I was not myself, was therapy. Long talks with a wonderful doctor, a slow climb to a medication regimen that worked.

'Tell me about your childhood,' my doctor asked on my first visit. I gave her a truncated version.

'I grew up in Hamilton and moved away for school.'

'Why did you want to move away?' she asked.

I shrugged. 'I wanted to see other places. Live in other cities.'

'Did you want to come back?'

'No.'

'Why not?'

I couldn't answer, not at first.

'Let's go back to your childhood,' she said. 'I want to know more about that.'

Why is my childhood important? I thought initially. It was over. It was finished. I'd travelled as far from it as I could.

But I hadn't travelled far enough. I'd moved on from it, physically and emotionally, and I'd tried to do the same with my disability, without realizing that the two were inexplicably intertwined.

I'd travelled *away* from all of it. My childhood and disability both. Now I needed to travel *through* them all over again to truly understand what it meant to have a body like mine, to be me, in the world.

These years later, I feel like I'm still discovering the answer, still writing this story anew.

In the penultimate episode of the HBO series *Game of Thrones*, the Dragon Queen, Daenerys Targaryen, wreaks havoc on King's Landing, the city she has come to conquer. Hers is a mission of revenge and redemption; she intends to reclaim the throne that was stolen from her family twenty years before. Riding atop her dragon, Drogon, Daenerys lays waste to the city and its people. She evades the defences that have been put in place to kill her and her dragon and then, after the city's armed forces have surrendered, proceeds to light the rest of the city – and its innocent civilians – on fire.

It was a twist that shocked – and infuriated – many a viewer. In the mythology of the show – which extended well beyond the mythology of George R. R. Martin's original books – Daenerys had been put forth as an archetypal protagonist over the course of eight seasons. She was a queen, beautiful though bruised, a kind-hearted yet steely ruler who freed slaves and garnered a grateful army eager to defend her. (Arguably, given how ready she was throughout the course of the show to burn and kill her enemies, her steeliness was itself suspect, hardly making her the kind ruler everyone longed for her to be.) Though her family line had been littered with madness – *every time a Targaryen is born, the gods flip a coin*, went the saying in the show – viewers had all hoped that the arc of Daenerys's character would take her away from that part of her history.

Fan backlash to the burning was swift, with multiple frustrations voiced on Twitter, Quora, and countless other platforms. In an article for *Nerdist*, writer Lindsey Romain puts it this way: '[The revenge] hinges her carefully deployed conquest on the unpredictability of feminine desire.'

The spectre of madness raises an additional question. In writing an episode where a female character with a family history of mental illness suddenly snaps under her rage, is the show – and its narrative – playing into the gendered ideas of *bitches be crazy* that people like *Alt-Minds*'s Kelly Aiello and others caution so strongly against? What does it mean, in today's storytelling world, to have a depiction of rage that is so closely tied to stereotypical beliefs around the pathology of female anger and mental illness?

Or perhaps we should be asking this question: what does it mean to have these stereotypical beliefs about female anger and unpredictability – and from there, stereotypical beliefs about insanity and its permutations – in the first place? How do the stories that we tell reinforce these ideas, and what exactly is it about these stories that society returns to again and again? How do these stories help to reinforce power structures that we chafe against and also acquiesce to at the same time?

It's only a story – except when it isn't. Except that people say this and eat these narratives and internalize that this is really how the world works: not the collective triumph, but the individual one; not society's responsibility to overcome the hostile world, but the narrator's responsibility to evade it. Individual responsibility, and also individual failure.

In today's world, the stigma that surrounds mental illness perpetuates the idea that this is not society's problem to fix. We might not expect dragons but we do caution against unpredictability, and these unpredictable individuals are isolated in much the same way as the individuals who were isolated in institutions centuries ago. Whether socially or otherwise, the exclusion of those with mental illness sets a framework for how these stories are viewed both in 'real' life and in the stories we see onscreen. On some level we expect Daenerys to go mad even if we don't want her to, because we've been told that that's what happens to women with power – that they cannot be trusted with it (the Evil Queen, the Wicked Witch), that they aren't meant to rule unless there's a husband by their side.

(Of course, the real world gives us plenty of stories featuring excellent female rulers – but these aren't the stories we tell before the fire, or on our pages, or on our screens.)

We expect the person with schizophrenia to be frightening and untrustworthy because that's how schizophrenia is portrayed onscreen and in popular story.

We see depictions of depression on television – someone who can't get out of bed, who can barely function – and tell ourselves that since our lives aren't that bad, we obviously can't be depressed. We don't need help. We are okay.

What would it mean to begin to tell a different kind of story? If Daenerys Targaryen, Mother of Dragons, was not left isolated and alone in that episode but had the support of the community around her, what might have been different?

'Angela Carter,' notes Marina Warner, 'called the spirit of the fairy-tale "heroic optimism," a better phrase for the promise of the happy ending.'

What might that promise mean if it's something we begin to build and share collectively, instead of something that one individual is solely responsible for bringing about?

What happens, in the story, when we reach out for each other?

Those three years of depression were the worst years of my life – and yet, in the end, I was lucky. I managed to connect with a good doctor; the cost of my therapy was covered by provincial insurance. After a prolonged period of therapy and the start of a medication regime that I continue to this day, I was able to move back into some semblance of my old life. I had family and friends and a support system that had been there for me all along – I had just been unable to see it.

I am also white, and I would be remiss if I did not acknowledge how that privilege played into my recovery. For every individual who connects with resources to help them with their mental health, there are countless others – many of them from IBPOC, disabled, and other marginalized communities – who never get the help they need. They are often not seen as palatable patients – medical professionals deem that they don't act the part of the grateful protagonist, or they are not connected to community in the way that I was, or racism on the part of the therapeutic community downplays or outright ignores their symptoms, or any one of countless other reasons that keep people from the resources they need.

Once again we place the onus of recovery – successful completion of the quest – on the individual, and place much less emphasis on the role and responsibility of the community to offer the help that it can. Once again, we support and perpetuate a culture where the emphasis is on the cure rather than societal change – where the aim of the narrative is to eradicate the disabled life rather than change the world so that the disabled life can thrive.

The stories we tell need to be different. It is no more and no less than that.

The physical nature of a disability is only part of it. The part you can see. The physical pain has an end, or at least moments of respite, however small; the mental preoccupation has hands that won't let go. See that imperfection, there. See that stumble. See that fall. See those crippled, folded toes. The scars on belly, back, and ankle. Feel the loops of that plastic shunt that now rests coiled in your abdomen – small tubes, like spaghetti, that sit just beneath the skin.

See how much time you waste thinking about these things in the first place.

How much of who we are is physical, and how much a product of the mind? When you wake up with arches that throb in pain, how do you ignore the way that shapes you? How do you account for the way failed dreams might push you elsewhere, make you search out other things?

Recently I've noticed that I've begun to walk with my feet turned in again. New shoes show signs of wear, even with my new orthopaedic inserts. The doctors tell me this is because I hit the ground hard – because I walk like someone who has learned to move with muscles that don't always pay attention. The slight circle of that right leg. The slap of that less-than-responsive right foot. These are called *coping responses*. The way the body picks up and compensates for a lack of proper motion. Evolution on the ground, so to speak.

A small child learns she won't be able to dance across that stage, not the way she might want. Instead she looks to words – to the warp and weft of a sentence, to the way that punctuation might shimmer on the blank stage of the screen. She finds rhythm in her letters, in the way that *this* letter paired with *that* letter paired with *these* makes a kind of music, on the page and on the tongue.

'Perhaps,' mused the poet Patrick Friesen in a 2013 essay published in the *Winnipeg Review*, 'this is true for all artists; you work at your second-favourite art form.'

And: '[I]f this is true, one should be able to spot the foundation of the favourite form within the art one is engaged in.'

And: 'Motion has always been at the core of what I do with words, and often this motion takes a musical direction … It means working with pacing. And it means speaking from the body instead of from the head.'

What does that mean, to speak, to write, from the body? Or, more specifically, what does it mean to write from a body such as mine? In my tweens my mother put me into dance class so that I could work on my balance. I loved dance and also hated it. It was a constant reminder of the dancer I would never be.

In my time as an undergraduate, I joined a Lindy hop class, then left when my dance partner joked about how I was concentrating so much and taking everything so seriously. The year after that first Lindy hop class, I joined another, and also left; I joined salsa classes in St. Andrews when I went to Scotland for grad school, and eventually left those classes, too. While living in Edinburgh I advertised for and found a swing dance partner who was patient and kind and perfectly willing to spend hours helping me stumble through my mistakes – I got excited about the dancing for a while, and then stopped scheduling sessions. (I signed up for more classes when I moved home to Canada, and left those ones, too, as soon as I found a viable excuse.) I was never going to be good enough. I was never going to be the dancer I wanted to be, and so I stopped. Again and again and again.

This seems like a silly reason now. But sometimes it's the silly, small decisions that have the greatest power. Instead of dancing, I sat down and wrote about dancing. Instead of *doing*, I sat down and dreamed.

Cerebral: of or relating to the brain. *Palsy*: muscle paralysis, or the inability to act.

Literally, when looked at in one light, a brain that paralyzes the body.

Monsters and Marvels

I was not born a superhero. I was born a mutant, and gifted a body unruly and strange. A twisted foot, a limp. A young girl who took her time to walk, a child who couldn't dance as others did. My early surgeries, wheelchair, and crutches marked my childhood in the same way that spider bites and accidents have marked our comic-book and big-screen heroes, except without any of the attendant power. I did not develop superhuman coordination in response to lopsided hips. Didn't find my eyesight sharpened or my hearing increased to compensate for less-than-stellar muscular performance.

Marvel: as a noun, a miracle or event that causes astonishment and surprise. Also, a wonderful story or legend. As a verb, *marvel* comes from the Old French *merveillen*, which means to be filled with wonder. The connecting verb is the Old French *merveillier* – to wonder at, be astonished.

Always the wonder, always the surprise. With superheroes, and then, also, with disabled people. Surprise when disabled people wheel down the street, when they struggle onto public transportation with a cane and walker, when they go to the movies, when they get groceries. *All by themselves.*

I don't know how you do it, passersby have said to disabled friends of mine, wheelchair users, those with canes. *If I were you, I would have killed myself a long time ago.*

Surprise. People were surprised by the bearded lady at the circus, by the dwarf who danced atop the bear. They came in droves in the late nineteenth century to see the deformities of Joseph Merrick, forever known to history as the Elephant Man. In the sixteenth century, they came to the French court to see Petrus Gonsalvus, originally from Tenerife, Spain, who had a hypertrichosis universalis mutation that made him excessively hairy. Petrus lived at court as a pet of the French king, Henry II. He was taught to speak Latin and dressed in fine clothes. Catherine de Medici, the queen, found him a wife, also named Catherine. (Portraits of them, thought to have influenced the image of the Beast in de Villeneuve's *Beauty and the Beast*, are still stared at in museums.) They had seven children, five of whom also bore the mutation.

His daughters were called monsters, marvels, beasts.

As a young girl growing up in southwestern Ontario, I found royalty easier to believe in than mutation, mutant though I was. Stories of princesses and kings were what I saw in books and on TV, and so I did not think about what it might mean to be a superhero, to tell that kind of story. Princesses were always perfect, and perfect was what I longed to be.

Superheroes required an entirely different kind of magic. It was easier to believe in the magic of fairy godmothers than to believe in the possibility of superhuman strength. Easier to believe that a girl might grow up and fall in love with a prince than to believe that that same girl might grow up into a body that might be considered beautiful, that did what she wanted it to do all of the time.

You walk like you have a pickle stuck up your ass, the children said to me at school. *Pickle! Pickle! Pickle! What are you going to do – pull it out AND EAT IT?*

Marvel: a comic-book universe. The franchise began in 1931 under the mantel of Timely Comics and rebranded as Marvel in 1961. The franchise oversees some of the most beloved superheroes and superhero teams in the world today: the Avengers, the Guardians of the Galaxy, Iron Man, the Hulk. Captain America. The X-Men. Spiderman. Deadpool. Dr. Strange. Thor.

Captain Marvel. She is a blond woman, young and pretty. Thin and stylish – someone who can wear a skin-tight armoured suit as easily as a baseball cap and leather jacket. She takes no prisoners, and after a brief beginning of uncertainty, mired in amnesia, makes no prisoner of herself. Once a fighter pilot, she now commands the space between the galaxies. Her name, when we first meet her, is Vers. She is not a princess, not exactly. She's something else – something bigger, larger, more.

Captain Marvel, née Carol Danvers. The latest iteration of Captain Marvel, a character who dates back to the Silver Age of comics. Previously, all iterations of the character were male. As I write this, in early April 2019, the Carol Danvers version of the character is – according to a 2016 *Vulture* interview with Kevin Feige, president of Marvel Studios – currently slated to become the most powerful superhero in the Marvel Universe. (We are several weeks out from *Avengers: Endgame*. Tickets for the first screening of *Endgame* sold out within minutes.) I saw *Captain Marvel* right when it came out, earlier this March. I loved everything about it – the sarcasm, the power, the joy. How refreshing to see a woman delight in her powers that way – how gleeful, how astonishing, to see someone rejoicing in the death meted out by her hands. How unbelievably powerful to see Brie Larson, as Carol Danvers, look

Jude Law's Yon-Rogg straight in the face and say, *I have nothing to prove to you*.

What might it have felt like, back when I was ten, to say those words to my classmates and know that they were true?

But then, I'm getting ahead of myself. A superhero narrative – or a fairy tale – means nothing if there's no adversity to overcome.

'The ideology of ability,' notes Tobin Siebers, 'is at its simplest the preference for able-bodiedness. At its most radical, it defines the baseline by which humanness is determined, setting the measure of body and mind that gives or denies human status to individual persons. It affects nearly all of our judgments, definitions, and values about human beings, but because it is discriminatory and exclusionary, it creates social locations outside of and critical of its purview, most notably in this case, the perspective of disability.'

In Angela Carter's short story 'The Bloody Chamber,' her gothic retelling of the Bluebeard fable, our young unnamed narrator begins the tale newly married to a much older French marquis. She doesn't love him but is drawn to him nonetheless; she shrugs off her misgivings about his previous history – three wives, all dead, the latest gone only three months when our narrator meets him – and is drawn to his magnetism, his wealth, and her own seeming power over him.

'When I said that I would marry him, not one muscle in his face stirred, but he let out a long, extinguished sigh. I thought: Oh! How he must want me!'

On her wedding day, the narrator, wearing her wedding ring (an heirloom first given to her husband's ancestor by Catherine de Medici), is brought by train to the castle where her libertine husband lives. It is gigantic and hollow and huge, filled with servants who disdain the narrator but put up with her as they have with so many of their master's whims. Their marriage's consummation, transpiring in 'broad daylight,' awakens both her disgust and her desire: 'I had been infinitely dishevelled by the loss of my virginity,' she says. Yet her husband then informs her that he must leave on business that very night, leaving her with her 'dark newborn curiosity' and a ring filled with keys. The key to his office, the kitchens, the study. On and on and on until there is only one left.

'One single key remained unaccounted for on the ring and he hesitated over it; for a moment, I thought he was going to unfasten it from its brothers, slip it back into his pocket and take it away with him.'

But the Marquis doesn't do this. Instead, he asks his bride not to enter this one last room.

'"Every man must have one secret, even if only one, from his wife," he said …. "All is yours, everywhere is open to you – except the lock that this single key fits."'

The husband leaves on his journey, and our narrator tries, at first, to distract herself with the rest of the castle. She is an accomplished pianist, a prodigy, and her husband has paid for the blind young piano tuner from a nearby village to come and take up residence at the castle solely to keep the narrator's instrument in tune. They strike up a friendship. The boy is sweet and kind.

But our narrator, alas, cannot forget the room. She ventures down into the bowels of the castle and finds that last locked door. Inside it, she discovered the bodies of her husband's last three wives. In her terror she drops a key into the pool of blood on the floor and then, after escaping from the room, discovers that the blood has stained the key.

Her husband, having completed his business early, is on his way back to the castle. Terrified at the wave of anger that she knows will come, the narrator finds herself abandoned in the castle, as the servants have left her alone – abandoned by all, that is, except for the lovely blind piano tuner, who stays with her to the end, a friend to be there with her as she meets her end at the hands of her husband.

But then, just in time, she is rescued. As the narrator's enraged husband accosts her at the front of the castle, the gleam in his eyes and fanatical voice hinting at her final end among the bodies in his basement chamber, the narrator is saved – not by the sweet young blind man, who remains innocent and useless, but by her mother, who has hastened to her daughter out of a creeping sense of fear for her safety and who comes charging up the causeway to the castle on a horse, her pistol held high and aimed perfectly at the evil husband's heart.

The Marquis dies; the narrator inherits the castle and gives it away to a school for the blind. At the end of the tale, she lives with her mother and the blind piano tuner in a little music school on the outskirts of Paris.

One doesn't often think of a mother when one thinks of a superhero, but Angela Carter was good at subverting expectations – in certain ways, at least. Her blind piano tuner is portrayed the way that most disabled bodies are, on the screen and on the page. If not monstrous and evil, then pitiful and useless, sweet though their souls might be.

It does not do, it would seem, to be subversive in more than a few ways at once.

Steve Rogers, in the context of his life before World War II, could perhaps be said to have a disability. At the least, his physical reality at the start of his narrative as Captain America in the Marvel films is an impediment to progress; he wants to be a soldier, but his big heart is no match for the smallness of his form. His is not a body in demand – he isn't *useful* by the standards of war and so he is overlooked, ignored, laughed at, forgotten. His desire to fight in the war is seen at best as cute, at worst as laughable. *I can do this all day,* he says at the beginning of his journey, as he faces off with a group of bullies in an alleyway. The bullies laugh because they know how society sees him – pitiful and useless, despite the vastness of his soul.

Look at you, they might as well be saying. *Still wanting to be a soldier!* (Still going out into the world, still doing things, still watching movies.) *I don't know how you do it. If I were you, I would have killed myself a long time ago.*

'From a narratalogical standpoint, it is not surprising that a genre so often associated with magical or extraordinary abilities portrays disability with such great frequency.' Ann Schmiesing is speaking of fairy tales here. But she could just as easily have been speaking about the superhero narrative – which is, after all, nothing more than the fairy tale updated for the twenty-first century. Instead of a ball gown, a superhero's cape. Instead of a pumpkin, a jet. Good triumphs here, too, and order is restored. A happily-ever-after with technology and modified bodies – a spider's bite, then a genetic mutation – taking the place of a magic wand or spell.

As a disabled woman, I don't know what it means to have your body represented onscreen in a way that isn't somehow tied to magic. If the disabled body isn't evil or mistaken (the hairy Beast, the green skin of the Wicked Witch, the disfigured face of Red Skull), it is always redeemed in the end – either through actual magic, as when the Maiden Without Hands has her hands grow back, or, as for many superheroes, through the magic of the compensation theory of disability. Daredevil loses his sight but develops supersonic hearing as a response to this bereavement; Charles Xavier of *The X-Men* loses the ability to walk but grows ever more powerful in the realm of the psychic mind. Jean Grey, a.k.a. Dark Phoenix, is ostracized and shunned because of how people's *marvelling* turns into fear – but her powers are extraordinary, so in the end it balances out.

Steve Rogers doesn't really have a disability in the strict sense of the term. His disability is only a metaphor – a slight against the unfair nature of the world in which he lived, a commentary on the preposterous idea of sending bodies off to fight wars in the first place. Even so, the serum that transforms him into a superhuman is a double act of erasure – erasure of the body that once was his and is no longer important, and erasure of the lived reality of those whose own bodies are seen to be an impediment to thriving. It is *useful*, for purposes of the superhero narrative, to see how the sheer force of Rogers's soul is matched in the end by his physique. But what does it mean to know that Steve Rogers's capacity for doing good is only reached once he is given a body that speaks to his soul's power? What does it mean, as a disabled person, to watch Steve's struggle and realize that your own potential will never be fulfilled in the eyes of the world – to realize that the world expects so much less from you as a result of your body that even the simplest of actions is treated like a galactic event? A broken body with a bright, pure soul. A superhero who is a superhero simply for getting up and getting coffee down the street. The disabled body is *less*; the disabled body must therefore be content with less, no matter how bright one's soul might be shining.

Look at you, getting coffee, getting groceries, going on trips in an airplane. Pretending that you're as able-bodied as the rest of us! It's all just so inspiring.

At the beginning of *Captain Marvel*, Carol Danvers is disabled in several ways. She has amnesia and can't recall her life beyond the six years immediately preceding her present. As the film progresses, we come to understand that she is also intentionally being disabled by her captors, the Kree, who are dampening her powers by keeping them artificially restrained.

But Carol, as most superheroes are wont to do, wrestles her way through to a happy ending. She does this both physically – through wreaking joyous, unrestrained havoc on her enemies – and emotionally, by distancing herself from the wild, perseverant machinations of Yon-Rogg and asserting her right to occupy her body and power in whatever way she sees fit.

I don't have anything to prove to you.

I don't have anything to prove to you.

I don't have anything to prove to you.

I whisper the same thing to myself at night. The 'you' wears many faces.

Once, while I was sitting at my desk during lunch period in fifth grade, a student sitting beside me asked if I could reach under my seat to grab her pencil, which had rolled under my chair.

'She can't,' my red-haired nemesis said behind me. 'She'll have to bend over and take the pickle out of her ass first.'

The rage that came over me was immediate and hot, overwhelming. I slammed my chair back into her desk so hard that it tipped her own desk over, pushing her so the chair she sat on teetered back on its hind legs. Wobbly and ready to collapse, exactly the way I felt. Her laughter was immediate, tinged with surprise and a sliver of terror. I heard the rest of the class laugh, too. Twenty-seven years later, I can close my eyes and hear that laughter exactly as it sounded on that day so many years ago.

I have never wanted to be a superhero, or a demon, something other than I was, as much as I did in that moment. To push the chair away from my desk and turn around and send that girl sweeping up through the air and back against the wall so hard that her skull cracked; to see her face split open upon impact and watch the blood and the brain matter trickle out down her cheeks. I wanted to stand over her as she screamed and grind her face into the floor. I wanted to turn an arm back toward the rest of the class who had laughed with her – who had always laughed with her – and do it to them, too. I wanted to see them cower, to see them lose themselves in awe. I wanted them to cry and scream and beg for mercy.

But I also wanted to be right to withhold that mercy – I wanted my anger to be justified, to make sense, to be understandable. To mete out punishment that was as clear and unbiased as that from a goddess. I wanted them to love me, to be terrified of me, to want to *be* me. I wanted all of this even though I knew, already, that in a few years I would go to a different high school and meet other people and move on from this part of my life. I wanted all of this even as I gasped in my rage and pulled my chair back up to its regular position and heard the girl behind me right her own desk and chair, her laugh shaky and hard. I wanted all of this through the rest of that afternoon as I stared at my desk red-faced and hot.

I wanted all of this through the next day, and the next, and the day after that one and the week after that. Limping through the hallways, limping through my life.

I have not stopped wanting all this.

Eventually I moved on to high school. I met other friends; life was indeed different. I travelled and lived in different cities and had lovers and felt beautiful and many of the things I had wanted came true.

I still have not stopped wanting all this. These triumphs, these vindications.

I go back, and back, to that day. I still want them to love me, even though I know it isn't worth it – even though I know, more importantly, that my anger and rage at the unfairness of it all is directly tied to the fairy-tale/superhero lens through which I was already, unconsciously, viewing the world. If my world was unfair, surely that meant that things would swing back around eventually. Surely events would put themselves to rights, surely I would get my happy ending, too, even if it took a little while – because isn't that what happened in all of the stories I was told? Life could be unfair but the world itself was a fair place. Be good, do good work, and you would either be rewarded or find the strength within yourself to put your world to rights. That's just how it went.

I didn't fantasize, back then, about what the world might look like if it actually was fair, if there was no need for super-heroes at all. I didn't imagine what life might have been like in a world without bullying. I took it for granted that the bullying would come, because I walked differently and occupied a different space and the world I lived in told me that was what happened to bodies that were different. It seemed easier to imagine a world where I had magical powers than a world where different bodies just existed together side by side.

The arc of the moral universe is long, but it bends toward justice. In an article for NBC's *Think* on the famous quote from Martin Luther King – a quote that was itself inspired by a sermon by the nineteenth-century clergyman Theodore Parker – writer Chris Hayes notes, 'The claim expresses a specific kind of informed optimism, an eyes-wide-open faith in humanity. Obviously, there is evil and trial and tragedy and hatred all around us and yet good, ultimately, does prevail. In the same way you can't tell the earth is round as you walk on it, the trajectory of history is imperceptible as we struggle through it; but rest assured its contours are there.'

What happens, though, when your eyes have never been wide open in the first place? If you are a disabled person whose life has been one sidelined narrative after another – the disfigured witch or the monster or the dwarf, the ill child as beatific sacrifice so that her parents might see God and better themselves – where is the moral arc of your own story?

The arc of the moral universe bends toward justice, but sometimes that arc takes a preposterously long time. And in the world we've built, it's easier for us to imagine that only superheroes – or perhaps fairy godmothers — can bend the arc for us. Everything else just takes too long.

What might it have meant to me – at eight years old, at ten – to know, deep in my bones, that I didn't have anything to prove to the classmates who told me that I walked funny, who sneered at the way I ambled through class? To understand that I wasn't waiting to become a princess or a superhero or even waiting for an unconventional rescuer, but instead was not in need of rescuing at all because there was nothing wrong with my body?

What does it mean for me now, at thirty-seven, to understand that the world still sees my body in this different way? As a disabled woman, I am at once hyper-present and completely invisible. My limp can at times be mild, and so I can sink into the background – an undercover agent in the able-bodied world, which is a kind of superpower and disguise that doesn't feel quite right, although it feels better than those long-ago days at school. My disabled body, bereft of both fairy godmothers and superhero change, is either an object of pity or an object of tender fascination, but rarely something other than that. We are sad Tiny Tims or we are *everyday superheroes*, inspiring those who can walk and run just fine with our inhuman strength in completing the impossible ordinary. Shopping in our wheelchairs, walking with our canes. Navigating the world with our guide dogs and scooters and other supports – augmentations that aren't sexy like the claws that come racing out of Wolverine's hands or the arc reactor in Ironman Tony Stark's chest or the impossible body that gets to be Steve Rogers's, but are nonetheless that we use to make ourselves be more.

Building a world that either accommodates these tools or makes it so the tools aren't necessary in the first place (why the need for a body that can fight wars if you build a world where there are no wars?) is a particular kind of magic, it would seem. One that still eludes us all.

A little over two years ago, I walked to work at the hospital one day and felt, as I battled the wind, the familiar words that pound through my head on a regular basis, in rhythm to my lopsided, hurried gait.

You *don't* walk *like* every*body* else.

YOU DON'T *WALK* LIKE *EVERY*BODY *ELSE*.

It's not unusual, this refrain. I think it every time I hear my footsteps on the ground. I hear it every time I catch my body passing by a window. And yet, for some reason, that day something changed.

It's not that you don't walk like everybody else, the little voice continued. It was my voice speaking something I had known all along.

It's that no one else in the world walks like you.

Why did it take me thirty-five years to realize this? Something to do with the way we tell stories – something to do with how we understand the body in both its regular variety and in what we perceive as its superhuman form.

'We are capable,' writes Tobin Siebers, 'of believing at once that the body does not matter and that it should be perfected.' And so we fantasize about eradicating disability in the same way that we fantasize about superheroes and magic – taking it for granted that the different body is aberrant in the same way superheroes are aberrant, gifts though these differences may be; longing for an act through which we will individually restore the world because systemic overhaul is too grand an undertaking. We're all for subverting stories until the subversion requires a change in the real world that involves work, at which point we fall back to our regular narratives and look to the one who'll come to rescue us. We take it for granted that the world is flawed and in need of a Captain Marvel to save it; we take it for granted that the disabled body is a bug in the system and do not, instead, celebrate its difference as a feature.

But my walk, my legs, my body – I am, *all* of me, a feature. (We are, all of us, a feature.) I have no fairy godmother because I have no need of one. I am not waiting for an unconventional white knight to come crashing up a causeway to my castle because I have seen the castle and its darkest heart and nothing in it scares me anymore. I have no need of rescue. I want more than the stories that posit the strong as those who survive and protect the rest of us. I want stories where people are not applauded for embracing difference but instead reshape the world so that difference is the norm.

I have nothing to prove to the world because the world has everything to prove to me. It is the world's responsibility to make space for my body, my words, my lopsided gait – our bodies, our words, our ways of moving through the world – to hold my childhood dreams of being a princess and a superhero close and help me understand that there is no need to want to be either. To start telling different stories about a body that might just look like mine, and reshaping the world to fit them.

I am already enough. There is no need to be more.

It appears that there is a leg length discrepancy, but none specific has been determined. She has right ankle clonus, an extensor plantar response on that side, but the deep tendon reflexes otherwise are not increased. I measured the calves equally, but I did think that the right foot was smaller than the left. The arm and hand on the right side appear normal and facial movements are symmetric.

I reviewed the accompanying CT and MRI scans (which have been returned with the family). The initial CT examinations show asymmetric dilatation of the cerebral ventricles, the left lateral one being larger than the right. On cursory viewing, it would appear that the child has a mild left lateral ventricular dilatation in association with porencephaly.

Porencephaly: derived from the Greek, meaning 'holes in the brain.'

However, historically there is no particular reason why she should have that problem. On further examination of the CT studies, and more particularly, the subsequent MRI views, it would seem that Amanda has an intraventricular cyst lying amidships in the left lateral ventricle. I believe that the latter scan definitively shows a spherical mass with an appropriate wall and which appears to be lying entirely within the ventricular cavity. That would seem to rule out the possibility of a porencephalic cyst which is usually juxtaposed to the ventricle and often doesn't have a discrete 'membrane.'

The importance of all of this is that the nature of this lesion be precisely defined. I would thus agree that Amanda requires a traditional ventroculo (or cyst to) peritoneal shunt, with the object being to place the ventricular catheter within the cyst cavity. If that can be achieved, then contrast should be run through the ventricular catheter in the cyst in an effort to determine whether it communicates with the rest of the ventricular system. There is the possibility that the cyst is isolated from the ventricle and also effectively occluding the outflow from the ventricle itself. In the event that the cyst can either not be *cannulated, or is isolated, then it is quite possible that the ventricle will have to be explored and the cyst removed. The parents obviously wondered whether it might be neoplastic, but I believe that it is not and that it likely is of a congenital origin such as ependymal or arising from the solar plexus.*

Neoplastic: of or relating to neoplasm or neoplasms. A neoplasm is an abnormal growth of cells that multiply and grow out of sync with the cells around it. In layman's terms, it is called a *tumour*.

Ependymal: the thin lining of the ventricular system of the brain. The ependyma helps to produce cerebrospinal fluid, which helps to cushion and protect the brain, and acts as a reservoir for *neuro-generation*, that process by which nervous tissues and cells regrow and repair.

Solar plexus: a group of ganglia and nerves located in the abdomen, behind the stomach. The solar plexus, also known as the celiac plexus, is responsible for keeping the organs running smoothly and shifting the body's metabolism in response to stress.

Thirty-some-odd years later, as I go over my doctor's notes in the sun-filled warmth of my parents' house, it isn't hard for me to see poetry in here, and also a quiet kind of magic. A growth in the brain, deriving from the process by which cells regrow and repair, perhaps connected to another mechanism within the body that prepares an individual for disruption. A life that was meant to be one way but ended up growing into something else, carrying everything within itself necessary to weather the change.

But the fact that I have lived to realize and understand this is hardly an individual triumph, personal success and even superhero story though it might seem be. I am where I am because of my parents, who saw something unusual in that two-year-old's walk all those years ago; because of Dr. Humphreys and the countless other physicians who consulted and operated and monitored me through the long years that followed my surgeries.

I am where I am because of the universal health care in my country, which ensured I could undergo neurosurgery without leaving my parents in lifelong debt. (Because somewhere along the way, someone with power decided it wasn't fair for Jack and his mother to keep all of the wealth they stole from the giant.)

I am where I am because of those difficult days on the school playground, which taught me hard but valuable lessons about empathy and growth. (Because the goal isn't to climb to the top of the social order and become like the Emperor, but to dismantle the social order in the first place.)

I am where I am because a nurse in my workplace saw the changeling in my skin and pushed me to get help.

I am where I am because I grew up a storyteller, and understood the ways that stories can move and shape us even before I understood exactly how to tell them.

I told the family, said my surgeon in those long-ago notes to my GP, *that I would write you about this matter and they are going to think further upon the recommendations given to them.*

Sincerely yours, R. P. Humphreys, MD, FRCSC

I am where I am today because of the community that carried me through.

9

The Great Unravelling

'[Disability] has a long history of being placed in the service of discrimination, inequality, and violence.'

– Tobin Siebers

'Few people would argue ... that the fairy tale has become a very specific genre in our lives and has inserted itself in inexplicable ways so that many of us try, even without knowing it, to make a fairy tale out of our lives.'

– Jack Zipes

'Disability marks the last frontier of unquestioned inferiority because the preference for able-bodiedness makes it extremely difficult to embrace disabled people and to recognize their unnecessary and violent exclusion from society ... It is as if disability operates symbolically as an othering other.'

– Tobin Siebers

When you put these quotations together, it's possible to see how both fairy tales and the ideology of able-bodiedness have combined to impose a very particular structure on the world in which we live. It is a structure that begins in story but then stretches outward to encompass all aspects of disabled life – political, social, economic. We exist in a world where happiness is synonymous with *not being disabled* – anything less than this comes across as undeserving, simply through virtue of not meeting the able-bodied ideal.

We also exist in a world that more often than not sees happiness within a framework of romantic fulfillment. (The prince and the princess live happily ever after.) And while that romantic ideal has progressed somewhat in recent decades – the shift to non-heteronormative romantic pairings, for example – the romantic 'happily ever after' continues to dog the disabled community in very particular, peculiar ways.

In an essay for the *Huffington Post*, the queer Canadian writer and disability awareness consultant Andrew Gurza – creator of the *Disability After Dark* podcast on disabled sexuality – wrote about his decision to employ sex workers as a way of ensuring that his sexual needs were met. His essay was met with reactions that ranged from gleeful support through to pity, with someone sending him a Twitter direct message commenting on how unfortunate it was that he had to use sex workers and couldn't find a partner.

But Gurza's essay wasn't about pity – it was about empowerment. It was about how a different way of looking at the world could enable him, as a disabled man, to build a future for himself where all of his needs were met, rather than trying to fit into society's mould for him.

In a follow-up interview with August McLaughlin, creator of the *Girl Boner* podcast, Gurza reiterated the point. 'I think that access to sex work should be funded by governments for disabled people and should totally be an option if you want it to be.'

In this landscape, the disabled person is choosing the way to bring about their own fulfillment, aided by a society that helps to ensure this happiness by likewise ensuring that different options for happiness are supported and encouraged. There is no longer just a prince marrying a princess, or even a prince marrying a prince. Perhaps a prince lives with another prince for a while and then spends some time on his own in the city. Perhaps a princess who best knows her own needs reaches out to the harem to see that her needs are fulfilled. Perhaps the queen in the wheelchair marries no one because she doesn't need to marry to show that her life brims with joy.

Maybe the half-hedgehog, half-human boy doesn't need to have his hedgehog suit burned at the end of his story in order to gain the happiness he craves.

In some versions of 'Cinderella,' the stepsisters are known only by their cruelty. In the tale written by Charles Perrault, 'Cendrillon, ou la petite pantoufle de verre', the older stepsister's name is Charlotte; the younger stepsister, distinguished only by the fact that she is not quite as rude or spiteful as her sister (she still manages to be fairly cruel), is still nameless. They do not matter — it is only what they do that is important.

In Perrault's version, after Cinderella triumphantly puts on the glass slipper, the sisters and the stepmother beg for her forgiveness, and she grants it. The stepsisters are married off to two gentlemen in the royal court, and Cinderella is married to her prince.

In 'Aschenputtel,' the version collected by Jacob and Wilhelm Grimm — no fairy godmother here, but instead a hazel tree imbued with the spirit of Aschenputtel's dead mother, and a dove that grants her wishes — the stepsisters, once again nameless, cut their feet in order to fit into the glass slipper and gain the favour of the prince. The first sister lops off her toe. The second slices off part of her heel. Each time, the dove flies over the coach that is carrying the prince and the deceitful stepsister away and alerts the prince to the treachery.

The stepsisters do not succeed. They do not ask forgiveness either, nor are they forgiven. Instead, they try to worm their way into Aschenputtel's life as bridesmaids at her wedding. At the end of the ceremony, doves peck out their eyes.

In the Disney version of the tale, the stepsisters, Drizella and Anastasia, are drawn big and clumsy. They have prominent noses and big hands and feet. When Anastasia shoves her foot into the glass slipper, it is her ungainly big toe that causes the glass slipper to ricochet off her foot and nearly shatter on the floor. Cinderella's foot, by contrast, is drawn with the faintest suggestion of toes, as though even toes themselves are ungraceful and hideous.

In 2017, I attend a panel discussion at a writing conference. The panelists are both very famous, and very eloquent. But I spend most of the time looking at the female panelist's shoes. At this panel, she is wearing dark-red ribboned sandals with beautiful wedge heels; the ribbons criss-cross up her calves and tie in bows at a point just below her knees. Beautiful, like walking on clouds. A woman who can walk gracefully in shoes like this has a kind of power you can't penetrate – a kind of confidence that seeps out into the air and somehow becomes a cover, a beacon, a shield.

I'll never be able to wear shoes like this. It shouldn't feel like a defeat, but it does.

Here is a secret: I find it hard to imagine that the way I walk through the world could be seen as beautiful by somebody else, even though I like the way I walk now, even though I would rather be the person who moves in an unusual way than the person who blends into the crowd.

It's hard to imagine that mine is the kind of body someone might want to hold hands with while walking down the street. This uneven gait is *mine*, but who would want to be around it twenty-four hours a day? It's one thing to say that we all have different bodies, that we all move through the world in different ways. It's another thing to look at the world around you and see the stories that get elevated – the real-life fairy-tale romances, the beautiful people who smile at you from the magazine pages and the television commercials and the billboard signs that you drive past on the highway.

It's hard not to internalize this – to look at the television programs that fawn over the man who marries the woman who had an accident and comes down the aisle in her wheelchair and to listen to all the people around you who say, over and over, *What a noble thing he's doing! How* nice *of him to marry a woman in a wheelchair!*

It's hard to look at a catwalk and watch the models and not feel, somehow, inferior. It's hard to recognize just how much of this ableism I've been eating and breathing for so long.

It's hard, too, to acknowledge that I feel this way while also simultaneously existing in a place of enormous privilege. My disability affects all aspects of my life, but it is also relatively mild. I am able to access places that disabled friends of mine cannot. I get nervous when I climb stairs but I can do it; my fine motor skills can sometimes betray me but are more or less reliable; I have chronic pain but it isn't yet insurmountable. I can dance, I can run, and if I get enough sleep at night, I can more or less face the day.

But when you're a young girl on the playground at school and children are laughing at you because you have short hair and they think you're a boy; when your peers whisper that you're ugly because you don't walk the way they think you should; when you're mocked at school because you are so visibly *different* from everyone else – when these things hit you, the scars go very deep.

Are you sure it isn't a big deal? an editor asked me in a comment on an essay of mine published several years ago, when I tried to downplay my disability in the course of explaining it. *You had a physical impediment that gave you social anxiety. You had a hard time in school. None of this is easy.*

I read her words and cried – the same way, several years before, I had cried when doing research for the first essay I ever wrote about my disability, when I found the study on school bullying and cerebral palsy that I cite in this book.

I do not want to walk like everybody else. I do not want to be like everybody else.

But sometimes it feels like that's all the world wants you to be.

And yet let us consider, for a moment, the physics of the high heel. In normal walking stance, the body is perpendicular to the floor, at more or less a ninety-degree angle. When the heels are raised, the centre of gravity shifts. The back arches, bringing the centre of gravity higher. The chest and buttocks are thrust out to counterbalance this gravitational shift. The calves tighten. To maintain the stability of the heel-toe downward slant, certain muscles in the lower legs remain flexed at all times. This, coupled with the illusion of added height, adds to that power, and that reality.

Everything must work harder, be harder, be *stronger*, to maintain stability.

This is the magic of high heels – the body is working harder to do what would otherwise come naturally. What you see when someone walks in heels is the *effort*, even when it looks effortless. The poise and the grace and the quick, purposeful stepping – all of this is done in order that one might balance, in order that one might not collapse.

How much time does the disabled person spend trying to conform to society's expectation of what it means to be a body in the world, when it would be so much easier to move through life without conforming? How much time do we spend forcing our feet into shoes that we shouldn't have to fit into in the first place? So much effort for a world that decrees everyone should wear high-heeled shoes/walk upright/conform to neurotypical social standards. And on and on and on.

So much effort, and all of it unnecessary.

'Disability,' as Tobin Siebers reminds us, 'has served throughout history to symbolize other problems in human society.'

We turn disability into a symbol because it has been socialized to be *not useful* – a burden on society, an uncomfortable ending. If disability is instead seen in story as a metaphor, there is potential for the happy ending as the able-bodied world knows it to truly be achieved. If a disability is not a disability so much as a symbol of something else, then once that symbol is realized, the disability can go away.

Modern art, as Siebers has shown us, began, with artists like René Magritte, to question the old idea that beauty comes from balance. In much the same way, our modern understanding of the fairy-tale story – and stories in general – must begin to question the idea of the *lack-lack-liquidation* pattern as popularized by Vladimir Propp and other theorists. In fairy tales, as we have seen, disability often operates as an impetus back toward balance and the world of the ideal: if the disabled narrator can only successfully complete the quest, do what is required of them, and learn, their disability will be lifted from them and they'll occupy an abled space in the world once more. The disabled villain, by contrast, occupies a place of disability that is permanent and somehow warranted. They are at once bitter and angry because of their disability and also disabled because of their bitterness and anger. For the villain, it's a vicious cycle from which there is no escape.

But this conceptualization of disability – at best merely a metaphor for psychological ills that can be overcome, at worst a punishment or judgment that can be reversed through magical or spiritual means, though only if one deserves it – does a disservice to the actual lived experience of what it means to occupy a different body in the world. Disability isn't visited on us in response to a grand, overarching narrative plan, but rather is a lived, complex reality that reimagines the very nature of how we move through and occupy space. It both shapes and is shaped by society, and denying the lived reality of what it means to be a disabled body in the world denies the possibility of growth on the disabled person's terms.

This is my body, the child on crutches might say. The real objective is not to heal the body until it can walk unaided again (though, for some, that might be the goal), but rather to understand what it means to move through the world with *this* body – and for the world, in turn, to make the appropriate space and adjustments for what the different body might require. In a world like this, the disabled body isn't a bad thing. Further, while being disabled might entail pain and struggle, it can also entail happiness and joy – particularly happiness and joy that's tied to the disabled experience. Does an able-bodied person know and fully understand the freedom and abandon that comes from flying in a wheelchair down a ramp – as exemplified by the #RampJoy hashtag started by disabled dancer and activist Alice Sheppard? An able-bodied person might be able to understand some of this feeling – the wild rush, the sense of fun – but it is the nature of the disabled person's lived experience that fully lights this sense of freedom. It is the lived, mundane reality of life as a wheelchair user that makes this particular joy so special. In her memoir, *Too Late to Die Young*, Harriet McBryde Johnson puts it this way: '[W]e can in our own way play with sight and sound, combine rhythm and form, move in our chairs and with our chairs, and glide and spin in ways walking people can't.'

In a 2018 *Catapult* essay about her life with a feeding tube, writer Kayla Whaley says it like this: 'Seeing inside my gut, learning to recognize its patterns and moods, felt intimate in a way that was wholly unexpected but altogether a joy.'

In short, life in the disabled body has its own particular joys. Being disabled puts us on a level of intimacy with our own bodies that in some ways remains, ironically, inaccessible to the able-bodied. We do not have to be happy in spite of disability. We can be happy because of it.

In a world such as this, the disabled body can be a hero. And there needn't even be a quest for them to prove it.

Understanding the varied richness of the disabled life – this reality that a life can be filled with pain and also joyous, that it can be bright and beautiful while also filled with struggle – has vast political implications. Consider the recent controversy over the proposal to increase social media surveillance at the US Social Security Administration. A line item in the agency's 2019 fiscal year budget overview suggested increased monitoring of social media accounts in order to protect against fraudulent disability claims. Under a ruling like this, posting pictures on Instagram or engaging in activist-fuelled outreach on Twitter could be seen as grounds for denying a disability claim. If you're well enough to engage with the world on social media, the reasoning goes, then surely you're well enough to not be on disability benefits. Like the stories we've told about heroes and villains for centuries, the stories we've told about disability operate on the same old binary – disability means complete incapacitation or it means nothing at all.

You're either a good person or an evil one. There is no in-between.

But what might a world look like that reaches beyond this binary? What shape does our Western world have if it moves beyond the traditional fairy-tale structures we've known for so long?

It takes the shape of new stories like *Special*, the 2019 Netflix show created by Ryan O'Connell that features a gay man with cerebral palsy as its main character. O'Connell, who has cerebral palsy himself and is also gay, is candid about what his goals were for the show.

'I never wanted to identify as being a victim, and to have that in the show was very important to me,' he notes in an April 2019 interview with *Variety* magazine. 'I want people to stop feeling like we're something to pity, or that we need to be treated with kid gloves.'

It takes the shape of Mandy Mouse, a new character introduced into the British children's television show *Peppa Pig* in early 2019. Mandy Mouse is a wheelchair user. She will speak to many children who are wheelchair users themselves. She will also speak to those children who are not, but who now get to see the disabled body as just another body in the world.

It takes the shape of the inaugural International Face Equality Week, celebrated in May of 2019. It takes the shape of the 'I Am Not Your Villain' campaign, and of the #Disability-TooWhite, #ThingsDisabledPeopleKnow, and #DisabledAndCute hashtags. Of #DisabledPeopleAreHot, started by *Disability After Dark*'s Andrew Gurza.

In Canada, it takes the shape of disability organizers like Sarah Jama, and disability activists and writers like Dorothy Ellen Palmer and deaf writer Adam Pottle, and people like Kelly Aiello who work to create space for these different voices.

It takes the shape of disability justice, where the collective voice rises up to force the world to change.

Patty Berne is the co-founder and artistic director of Sins Invalid, a disability justice–based performance project, her 'Disability Justice – a working draft' can be found on the Sins Invalid website. 'A Disability Justice framework,' she writes:

> understands that all bodies are unique and essential, that all bodies have strengths and needs that must be met. We know that we are powerful not despite the complexities of our bodies, but because of them. We understand that all bodies are caught in these bindings of ability, race, gender, sexuality, class, nation state and imperialism, and that we cannot separate them. These are the positions from where we struggle. We are in a global system that is incompatible with life. There is no way to stop a single gear in motion – we must dismantle this machine.

We've come a long way from the time when we told magical stories in front of the fire as a way of making sense of disability in the world. We have prosthetic limbs and wheelchairs and eyeglasses that can correct to 20/20 vision. But so many of the stories and narratives we continue to tell argue that disability is a thing to overcome, to eradicate, to disappear. Stories like these are what fuel the difficulties that disabled people encounter in the world. When you are taught from the time you are a young child that the disabled body is weak and other, set apart, you partake in a world that seeks to entrench this *otherness* through systemic and cultural barriers. You participate in a culture, even unknowingly, that furthers disabled exclusion.

As we've seen with the stories, this type of learning starts early and works on many levels. One of the primary ways disabled exclusion operates is through language: our tendency to associate disability and disabled characteristics with weakness and inferiority influences the metaphors we choose and the words we use. Disabilities and conditions are co-opted for use as the ableist labels and descriptors that pervade our ways of speaking.

An unpredictable person is jokingly referred to as *schizo*; someone with mental illness is *mental, bonkers, bat-shit crazy*. Something (or someone) that disappoints is said to be *lame*.

People are *confined* to wheelchairs; they *succumb* to long illnesses, as though the strength required to fight said illness can't be mustered and giving in is somehow a choice; people who are ignorant of an issue are *blind* to it. Someone who isn't paying enough attention to the insensitivity of their language is *tone-deaf*. Bit by bit, the language we use reinforces the idea of disability as a thing of weakness, making the disabled person into someone weak, someone *less*.

And then there are the military metaphors. The military metaphor of illness (*lost the battle* with cancer, *fought long and hard* against AIDS) came to prominence in the early twentieth century, as a way of encouraging soldiers to guard against syphilis. If disease, and by extension disability, can be cast as the enemy in war, then all methods undertaken to eradicate it can themselves be cast in the light of what is good and right. If we are *fighting* against cancer, then gene therapy that eradicates cancer-causing mutations will be seen as a force for the good – so, too, for gene therapy that 'cures' blindness, or gene therapy that eradicates Down's syndrome, or prosthetics that allow a wheelchair user to walk upright and thus be 'free'.

When you are taught that the disabled body is bad, when you use language that reinforces this viewpoint – even and perhaps especially when you use that language unconsciously, without considering what it might mean to speak of someone's lived reality as a metaphor for a difficulty in your own life, or when you use this language to reinforce the idea, however well-intentioned, that the disabled person can and should rise above their physical limitations – you participate in a world that seeks to further entrench disabled exclusion.

Consider the cliché of *not letting your disability define you* – this is, at the very least, a dressed-up version of the military metaphor. If you *don't let your disability define you,* then the implication is that you've won: you've refused to allow your disability to run roughshod over your life; you've emerged triumphant from the battle and manage to go about your daily business and activities just like everyone else.

But what do we mean when we say we are defined by something? I was born with a body that didn't work as others' did – I have navigated my way through the world for my entire life steered by the fact that my body is different. I can't wear heels, I don't like stairs, I worry every day about living alone and losing my balance in the shower. Sometimes – increasingly, if I'm honest – I lose my balance simply walking down the middle of the street. My feet hurt, my legs hurt. I almost always have a head tilt in pictures. These days I am tired nearly all of the time.

Yet I am who I am because of this body and its lessons and learnings. I *am* defined by it. Every step I take is a reminder of how my physical reality is defined in the world.

But that's not it, someone might say. *You might* be *disabled, but you* aren't disabled. *You are a* person with a disability, *not a* disabled person*! You aren't letting it take charge of your life!*

Again – what does that mean? If I wake up one day and the fatigue and the migraines and the pain is so bad that I decide to go back to bed and sleep, is *that* when my disability defines me? Am I only defined by my disability if it gets in the way of going out and being productive in the world?

And if so, how productive do I need to be to ensure that I am not seen as someone who is being defined by this lesser idea of her body? How much is too little? Where do we draw the line – at someone who can work, at someone who can hold down a job, at someone who can interact with friends and family and be social on a constant basis so that they aren't *weird* or *unusual* or some other kind of name?

Susan Sontag on illness: '[T]he metaphoric trappings that affirm the experience of having cancer have very real consequences; they inhibit people from seeking treatment early enough, or from making a greater effort to get competent treatment.'

Similarly, the metaphoric trappings of the way that society talks about disability also have very real consequences. It means something to hear that *So-and-so doesn't let their disability define them!* when you have very bad agoraphobia and cannot leave your house; it means something to hear that the amputee who has just won an Olympic medal *doesn't let their disability define them* when you, perhaps, are an amputee who cannot do the hundred-metre dash. It places disabled people in constant competition with one another, encouraging us to prove that we are each more able-bodied than the next. It completely ignores the reality of our lives in favour of a fantasy that no one can reach.

Believing that someone is defined by a disability also carries with it an expectation of how we as people in general are supposed to move through society – how we're supposed to talk, to love, to make friends, to be productive. It carries a particular expectation of what it means to be a contributing part of society – and, hidden within this, an expectation that one must contribute to society in order to prove one's worth to the world. 'In the contemporary workplace,' writes Melissa Gregg in her book *Counterproductive*, 'productivity is encouraged as long as the worker's body is capable. When the same body is disabled, wellness services provide the healing necessary to resuscitate living labor.' If you are defined by your disability in such a way that it's deemed you can't contribute, then you aren't worthy. If you contribute in a way that's *less*, you are also worth *less* than others – at least until you can be 'rehabilitated' to operate on the same level as the rest of the workforce.

(This metaphorical *less* can be literal, too: – in the US, disabled people are allowed to make as little as one dollar an hour if their work is deemed less than that of their able-bodied counterparts. It's an exemption to the Fair Labor Standards Act and has been in place for eighty years.)

'Justice will be a long time in coming,' Sarah Jama notes. 'It's really not to the benefit of social structures that do exist to make concessions for disabled people because there's no economic value [in it]. In fact, the fear is that it will take away from society because you're literally training people to understand that they have worth outside of their ability to produce, which can dismantle entire structures.'

When you are blind and cannot drive a car, are you *letting your disability define you* by not driving? Is someone who lives with depression defined by that depression in a way that makes them less? Are disabled people who cannot compete in the Paralympics intrinsically worth less than disabled people who can? Are any of us, so 'defined' by our disabilities when they keep us from doing one thing or the next, less for being so?

Or are we just living our lives in a way that looks different from the norm? And when you train people to understand that they have worth simply through being who they are – that a life that is *different from the norm* has just as much value as any other life – what kind of world-shaking magic happens then?

'There is a profound respect,' writes Marina Warner, 'in the [fairy-tale] genre for what words do in the world, as well as in the stories.' A key part of disability rights lies in recognizing and respecting the power that our own words have in the world that we move through today. These fairy-tale stories we've been telling ourselves for thousands of years have never been *only stories* – in their language, in their focus on magic, in the modern fairy tale's push for the happy ending, they help to shape and inform our ideas of what it means to be happy and fulfilled. And they can continue to help us shape and inform our ideas of what it means to be happy and disabled in the world so long as we understand how the narrative of able-bodiedness – the prince and princess who look like everyone else — has woven itself into the story framework.

We must respect and understand what words do in the world so that we can begin to do the work of unmaking the fairy tales we've told about disability for so long – of cutting the thorns back from Sleeping Beauty's castle, or perhaps bringing the entire castle down stone by stone. Every time we speak in a way that positions the disabled body as less, every time we absorb a story about a girl or a boy who cannot walk and then is made mobile, or a neurotypical protagonist or a princess who gets everything she wants because she is *pretty* – every time we embrace the able-bodied happy ending – we allow the thorns to grow. Going forward, it is our responsibility to tear out the thorns so that something else can grow instead. To envision a fairy tale and a world where the environment isn't hostile – where the protagonist with the different body and the different way of being in the world can triumph not because of the obstacles they overcome on their own but because of the community that helps to pull them through.

To make space, in the end, for different stories.

Afterword

The day I finished writing this book, the last episode of the television series *Game of Thrones* aired on HBO. In the finale, Daenerys Targaryen, the Dragon Queen, is killed by her lover Jon Snow. The era of absolute monarchical rule is overturned in favour of a kingdom that looks slightly more like a democracy – a council of nobles votes to install Brandon Stark on the throne, with the next king or queen after him to likewise be chosen by vote.

Bran, introduced as a main character in the first season of the series, is pushed out of a window as a child and becomes paralyzed from the waist down as a result. His many adventures over the course of the series include fleeing to the North and becoming the Three-Eyed Raven, a seer who can access the vision of high-flying birds and can tap into all of history. Initially carted around on a wagon as a result of his disability, Bran is shown, in the latter seasons of the series, in a custom-made wheelchair. When he is crowned king, the wheelchair becomes his throne.

His name as king: Bran the Broken, First of His Name, King of the Andals and the First Men, Lord of the Six Kingdoms and Protector of the Realm.

It was a twist that hardly anyone saw coming. Like the twist that saw Daenerys Targaryen light King's Landing on fire, it was also a plot development that ignited fierce criticism from viewers, not least of all from the disabled community.

Bran the Broken. A man who would be king but must carry the perceived limitations of his disability in his very name; a man who has travelled far from his home and endured a great deal (all, it must be said, with the help of family and friends who support him in various ways through the show) and triumphed over many things, only to be brought back to this question of his body's inherent flaw right at the pinnacle of his achievement.

It's worth noting that the moniker of Bran the Broken is given to Brandon Stark by Tyrion Lannister, a character in the show who is a dwarf, played by actor Peter Dinklage. Some discussions in the disabled community in the hours after the finale aired centred on how the use of 'Bran the Broken' hearkens back to a line of Tyrion's from much earlier in the show, where he admits an affinity for 'bastards, cripples, and other broken things.' On her Twitter feed, Rebecca Cokley noted that in this context, the name Bran the Broken operates as an instance of cross-community solidarity – one disabled person speaking to another, both of them conscious of how the 'broken' label speaks to the physical reality of their lives and also reaches beyond this reality to proclaim that a broken man, as such, will be the one to knit these broken kingdoms back together.

Personally, I was pleasantly surprised by Bran's elevation to the throne. The use of the name Bran the Broken does seem problematic to me insofar as it operates on the same level as the disabled 'superhero' narrative, underscoring the inspirational nature of his ascent to the throne (A king! And a broken one! *Look how much he's overcome!*) in a way that would not be done for a king or queen who was able-bodied. No matter

Bran's accomplishments – at the end of the day he is still a man in a wheelchair, king or not.

But I'd be lying if I didn't also say that I liked how a disabled man – one who remains disabled throughout the show and doesn't encounter a magical cure despite the fantastical nature of the series – ends the series in a position of such power. I loved the fact that the kingdom necessarily begins to make adjustments for Bran; the famed Iron Throne having been destroyed by a dragon, the wheelchair becomes his de facto throne, and those who gather around him must necessarily make the space that the wheelchair requires. Of course, the treatment of his disability and his ascent to the throne isn't perfect – the resounding reaction of the disabled community to that episode went along the lines of *King's Landing is hella inaccessible!* – but the fact that a disabled body was put in a place of such power at all, and that it happened in a fantastical, fairy-tale-esque universe to boot, in such a wildly popular series – seemed hugely important to me.

The reality of the matter is that nothing is perfect in the disabled stories we tell, or the disabled lives we live out in the world, and capturing these imperfections is a key part of telling our stories properly. It is not possible for the disabled individual and the disabled life to have the happy ending that traditional fairy tales require, but the happy endings that we *can* have, and that we deserve, are much better. They are intricate and complicated, requiring both individual arcs and community support, individuals who change in order that the world itself can shift and improve to meet them head-on. They aren't happy endings so much as they are departures of varying degrees of positivity. There is always more work to be done. A traditional happy ending leaves this work entirely out of the picture.

Flawed as it is, it means something to have a show and story as big as *Game of Thrones* showcase disability in this way. It meant everything to me to see that story institute a new world with disability and the different body at its helm. And the fact that this story has the kind of cultural hold on our modern Western society we once gave to fairy tales seems to me entirely fitting – we may have grown beyond the scope of the fairy tales we once knew and loved, but their structure and their power still have a hold on who we are. They teach us valuable things about what it means to believe in something, to use the pleasure and power of stories to unite our different communities and bring us together.

Several weeks after the *Game of Thrones* finale aired, the actress Ali Stroker made history as the first wheelchair user to win a Tony award for Best Featured Actress. She won for her performance in the 2019 revival of the musical *Oklahoma!* Because the stage did not have a wheelchair ramp (despite the awards ceremony taking place at Radio City Music Hall, a venue that has reams of experience in building sets for shows and could thus presumably have built a ramp for a wheel-chair-using actress), she had to wait backstage until her name was called out, at which point she wheeled onstage to accept her award.

Later, when *Oklahoma!* won Best Revival of a Musical, she was the only member of the cast who was, once again because of the lack of a ramp, unable to go onstage to accept the award.

If society is used to not seeing disabled people in stories, society becomes used to not seeing disabled people in real life. If society is used to not seeing disabled people in real life, society will continue to build a world that makes it exceedingly difficult for disabled people to *participate* in said world, thus perpetuating the problem. In this world, there is no need for a wheelchair ramp because hardly anyone who wins an award will need one to get onstage. But what if we took it for granted that anyone, regardless of ability, might be able to achieve, and built our stages and our environments accordingly?

It is time for us to tell different stories.

It is time for a different world.

Give me a story about a disabled man or woman who learns to navigate the world and teaches the world, in turn, to navigate its own way around the disabled body. Give me power and also weakness, struggle but also reams of joy.

Our lives are made of this fabric – our stories deserve nothing less.

In her short story 'A Conversation with My Father,' Grace Paley has this to say about the way our lives move through the world: '[Plot is] the absolute line between two points which I've always despised. Not for literary reasons, but because it takes all hope away. Everyone, real or invented, deserves the open destiny of life.' Society has treated the disability narrative as this 'absolute line' for centuries – a very specific journey to an unhappy ending. Disability as the antithesis of able-bodied-ness; disability as something less and other. *Disability*, seen with this lens, obliterates the status quo of the able body and demolishes the happiness that society has traditionally associated with health and wellness. Disability, in this sense, becomes the very thing that takes hope away.

But the truth is that the disabled life and the disability narrative can be – and indeed are – filled with hope. Disabled people live lives filled with pain and joy and struggle as much as anyone else. To view literature through the lens of the 'open destiny of life' is to understand that the end of a story is not so much an *ending* as it is a *departure* – the point at which the audience stops travelling alongside the protagonist and allows them to continue their way through the world. In much the same way, we need to understand that the 'ending' of the disability narrative need not come with either a restoration of able-bodiedness or a descent into despair at the removal of able-bodied life. Instead, disability narratives and disabled lives deserve to continue as they are, moving forward equally into the realms of joy, frustration, sorrow, anger, and all of the other elements that make up the complex reality of living. We deserve the 'open destiny of life' as much as anyone else, and the stories we tell about disability deserve exactly the same.

Stories have a deep effect on children – and continue, whether we acknowledge it or not, to have a deep effect on the adults those children become. A disabled child who grows up on fairy tales and stories that either do not feature disabled protagonists or connect disability to a variety of impediments and failures becomes an adult who is used to seeing disability shrouded and hidden away from the realities of life. That adult thus comes to equate, whether consciously or not, the disabled life with the journey that stops and does not continue. The lack of positive disabled protagonists or characters in books and movies does not, in such a world, become cause for question or consideration. It becomes, simply, a fact of life. And so too do the unconscious biases that form as a result of being exposed to disability as a *character flaw*, as we are in many of the fairy tales we know in the Western world. Disability is a negative that is tied to impediment right from the very moments that we begin to understand story.

My own disability has been a fact of my life since I was three years old. I spent a great deal of time trying to ignore it

– to pretend that my limp and other difficulties weren't there. I did this because I did not see myself reflected in the stories I read or the movies I watched. When Ariel walked, she walked gracefully, and everything turned out all right for her in the end. Where were the stories or the fairy tales about little boys and girls in wheelchairs, or girls who limped when they tried to dance in ballet class? They didn't exist. Happy endings were only for the able-bodied. And so, since I most definitely wanted a happy ending in my own life, I set about pretending to be exactly that.

But my own fairy tale, the one that began with that first step into the hospital, has always gone a separate way. I came out of that hospital into a different life, and though I move through the world now in a mostly able-bodied way, I can't help but wonder how my life might have gone had I seen little girls – and yes, even princesses – in wheelchairs and on crutches early on in my years of development. How might my own view of myself as a disabled woman have grown in an environment like that? If I had read stories that encouraged the celebration of disability as just another element of life, how might my teen years have unspooled?

I might have been more vocal. I'd certainly have been more apt to include disability in the stories I was beginning to tell – more apt to see these differences as cause for celebration, yes, but also more apt to see these differences as *normal*.

Whether we acknowledge it or not, the stories we tell ourselves as children shape the world that we encounter. Fairy tales and fables are never *only stories*: they are the scaffolding by which we understand crucial things. Fairness, hierarchy, patterns of behaviour; who deserves a happy ending and who doesn't. What it means to deserve something in the first place; what happy endings mean in both the imagination and the world. As a writer, I have only just begun to understand how all this shaped my sense of fairness and equality – as a disabled woman, I have only now realized the power inherent in claiming that complicated happy ending for yourself even if the stories tell you otherwise.

When we tell stories, we look for happy endings as a way of reckoning with the unfairness of the world – with its injustice, with its cruelty, with its staggering ability to wear us down minute by minute. And yet a happy ending is made of a million things. Perhaps, for some, it is made of romantic love. Perhaps, for others – for myself – it is made of the kind of love that comes from that wellspring of the self, from the acknowledgement that what I've encountered throughout my life is not something to overcome on my way to happiness, but, in fact, the very fabric of my life's joy in the first place. I do not walk through the world like anyone else – but I'm proud of that now, even as it comes with its challenges, and I'm eager to see how the stories I tell can help others to uncover this same joy.

Once upon a time, a dark-haired little girl walked into a hospital and began a journey that came to define the way she saw and experienced the world. It was not the happy story she wanted as a child. Even now, as an adult, there are parts of the story that can hurt, and there are still times when I catch my gait in the mirror and feel a whisper of those voices that spoke so cruelly when I was a child.

But this is the fairy tale I get to tell. This is my complicated happy ending – my complicated, happy *life*. To pretend that any of this is something to overcome – as the world so often does – is to do myself and my community a disservice. Disability is something I live with, not something I've vanquished as if it's a villain. The stories I tell now try to show this. The stories we *all* tell now should try to make space for this truth in some way.

Give me a princess in a wheelchair. Give me a man who outwits an evil sorcerer not because of magic but because his mind sees the world differently, a condition that allows him to see outside himself and recognize that difference in other people. Give me stories where *disability* is synonymous with a different way of seeing the world and a recognition that the world can itself grow as a result of this viewpoint.

Give me fairy tales where disabled characters not only triumph but also change the world. Because disabled people have already done that countless times over, and in a world that continually tells them another story: one where they have no place at all. What might we accomplish, instead, in a space where the disabled body is front and centre in our stories?

When I tell stories now, when I use them to interrogate the world, I think of that girl from thirty years ago whose life went down a different path into the woods. Hers was a story that went sideways from what she'd imagined, but in doing so it became a story that could reach for a different, more difficult kind of happiness. When I read fairy tales now, I think of this.

I do not want a story that ends with an arc into the sea, but neither do I want a story where difficulties vanish and everything is *perfect*. None of us should want those things. Instead I want a story where a prince – where anyone, really – might find a way to communicate with a woman who has no voice. Where we understand and reach out for each other and are left, together, to confront the open destiny of life.

These, to my mind, are the fairy tales worth telling.

Notes

The author thanks Jeannine Hall Gailey for permission to excerpt her poem 'The Little Mermaid Warns You, You May Have Already Become Forgotten' (originally published in *Enchanted Living Magazine* [formerly *Faerie Magazine*]) as an epigraph. She thanks Patrick Friesen for permission to excerpt lines from his essay 'Poetry Was My Back-Up Plan, After Music' (originally published in the *Winnipeg Review*).

Chapter Eight, 'Monsters and Marvels,' was originally published as 'Monster or Marvel: The Disabled Life in a Superhero Universe' on LitHub, April 26, 2019.

Select parts of the untitled memoir sections in this book were originally part of the essay 'The Second Art Form,' published on The Rumpus on September 3, 2013.

Unless otherwise noted, definitions in this book are taken from the Merriam-Webster Online Dictionary.

Unless otherwise noted, historical definitions of words are taken from the Online Etymology dictionary, available at www.etymonline.com.

Unless otherwise noted, references to the tales in the Grimms' *Kinder- und Hausmarchen* are taken from *The Original Folk and Fairy Tales of The Brothers Grimm: The Complete First Edition*. This is the first English translation of the original volumes of the KHM published in 1812 and 1815. This translation was completed by Jack Zipes and published in 2014.

Where later editions of the tales are noted in the text, those readings were taken from *The Complete Fairy Tales of the Brothers Grimm, All-New Third Edition*, published in 2003. This text was also translated by Jack Zipes and taken from the 1857 edition of the KHM, the seventh and final edition to be published while the Grimms were still alive.

Works Consulted

Andersen, Hans Christian. 'The Cripple.' In *Hans Christian Andersen Fairy Tales and Stories*, translated by H. P. Paull. Denmark: 1872. hca.gilead. org.il/inkling/cripple.html

———. 'The Emperor's New Suit.' In *Hans Christian Andersen Fairy Tales and Stories*, translated by H. P. Paull. Denmark: 1872. hca.gilead.org.il/emperor.html

———. 'The Little Mermaid.' In *Hans Christian Andersen Fairy Tales and Stories*, translated by H. P. Paull. Denmark: 1872. hca.gilead.org.il/li_merma.html

———. 'The Ugly Duckling.' In *Hans Christian Andersen Fairy Tales and Stories*, translated by H. P. Paull. Denmark: 1872. hca.gilead.org.il/ugly_duc.html

———. *Hans Christian Andersen Fairy Tales and Stories*. Translated by H. P. Paull. Denmark: 1872. hca.gilead.org.il

Anderson, Kenneth et al. *Cinderella*. DVD. Directed by Clyde Geronimi, Hamilton Luske, and Wilfred Jackson. Manhattan: RKO Pictures, 1950.

Arabian Nights, The. Translated by Husain Haddawy. New York: W. W. Norton & Company, 1990.

Basile, Giambattiasta. 'Sun, Moon, And Talia.' In Multilingual Folk Database. February 14, 2019. www.mftd.org/index.php?action=story&id =3364

Barbarin, Imani. 'All My Life, People Have Told Me I'm "An Inspiration." Here's Why It's So Harmful.' *Bustle*, April 5, 2019. www.bustle. com/p/all-my-life-people-have-told-me-im-inspiration-heres-why-its-so-harmful-17004612

Barbot de Villeneuve, Gabrielle-Suzanne. 'Beauty and the Beast.' In *Junior Great Books*: Series 4, Book One. Chicago: The Great Books Foundation, 2011. humanitiesresource.com/ancient/articles/Beauty_and_ Beast-Final.pdf

The Bible, New Standard Version

Berne, Patty. 'Disability Justice – a Working Draft by Patty Berne.' Sins Invalid, June 9, 2015. sinsinvalid.org/blog/disability-justice-a-working-draft-by-patty-berne

Boden, Anna, Ryan Fleck, and Geneva Robertson-Dworet. *Captain Marvel*. DVD. Directed by Anna Boden and Ryan Fleck. Burbank: Buena Vista Pictures, 2019.

Bottigheimer, Ruth. *Fairy Godfather: Straparola, Venice, and the Fairy Tale Tradition*. Philadelphia: University of Pennsylvania Press, 2002.

Bourke, Angela. *The Burning of Bridget Cleary*. London: Pimlico, 1999.

Campbell, Joseph. *The Hero With a Thousand Faces*. Novato: New World Library, 2008.

Carter, Angela. 'The Bloody Chamber.' In *The Bloody Chamber And Other Stories*. New York: Penguin Books, 2015.

Changing Faces UK. 'I Am Not Your Villain.' November 16, 2018. www.changingfaces.org.uk/i-am-not-your-villain-campaign-launches-today-in-the-telegraph

Christensen, Jen and Leyla Santiago. 'Despite rhetoric, illness threat from migrants is minimal, experts say.' CNN, November 2, 2018. www.cnn.com/2018/11/02/health/migrant-caravan-illness/index.html

Clements, Ron and John Musker. *The Little Mermaid*. VHS Tape. Directed by Ron Clements and John Musker. Burbank: Buena Vista Pictures, 1989.

Crafton, Donald. *Before Mickey: The Animated Film 1898–1928*. Chicago: University of Chicago Press, 1993.

Dangerfield, Katie. 'N.S. teen with cerebral palsy pressured to lie in creek, walked on by classmate.' Global News, November 9, 2018. globalnews.ca/news/4647329/bullying-video-ns-teen-cerebral-palsy/

DePalma, Anthony. 'Father's Killing of Canadian Girl: Mercy or Murder?' *New York Times*, December 1, 1997. www.nytimes.com/1997/12/01/world/father-s-killing-of-canadian-girl-mercy-or-murder.html

De Beaumont, Jeanne-Marie. 'Beauty and the Beast'. *The Young Misses Magazine* (French Title: *Magasin des enfans, ou dialogues entre une sage gouvernante et plusieure de ses élèves*) Containing Dialogues between a Governess and Several Young Ladies of Quality Her Scholars, 4th ed., v 1. London: C. Nourse, 1783), pp.45-67. January 20, 2019.

De Villeneuve, Gabrielle-Suzanne Barbot, 'Beauty and the Beast'. *Four and Twenty Fairy Tales*, trans. J.R. Planché. London: G. Routledge and Co, 1858.

Dolmage, Jay Timothy. *Disability Rhetoric*. Syracuse: Syracuse University Press, 2014.

Dorwart, Laura. 'What the World Gets Wrong About My Quadriplegic Husband and Me.' *Catapult*, December 6, 2017. catapult.co/stories/what-the-world-gets-wrong-about-my-quadriplegic-husband-and-me

Editors of Encyclopedia Britannica, The. 'Ancients and Moderns.' *Encyclopædia Britannica*, January 29, 2015. www.britannica.com/art/Ancients-and-Moderns

Ellington, Tameka N. 'The Origin of Anansi the Spider.' Paper presented at the International Textile and Apparel Association 2016 Conference: Blending Cultures, Vancouver, BC, September 2016. lib.dr.iastate.edu/cgi/viewcontent.cgi?article=1806&context=itaa_proceedings

Elliott, Ted, Terry Rossio, Joe Stillman, and Roger S. H. Schulman. *Shrek*. DVD. Directed by Andrew Adamson and Vicky Jenson. Universal City: Dreamworks Pictures, 2001.

Frainey, Brendan, Beverly Tann, Susan Berger, Melanie Rak, and Deborah Gaebler-Spira. 'Bullying in Children and Adolescents with Cerebral Palsy and Other Physical Disabilities.' *American Academy for Cerebral Palsy and Developmental Medicine*. Accessed January 5, 2019. www. aacpdm.org/UserFiles/file/SP14-Frainey.pdf

Friesen, Patrick. 'Poetry was my Back-Up Plan, After Music.' *The Winnipeg Review*, March 22, 2013.

Game of Thrones. Seasons 1-8. Created by David Benioff and D. B. Weiss. Aired April 17, 2011, on HBO. DVD.

Gilbert, Sophie. 'The Dark Morality of Fairy-Tale Animal Brides.' *The Atlantic*, March 31, 2017. www.theatlantic.com/entertainment/ archive/2017/03/ marrying-a-monster-the-romantic-anxieties-of-fairy-tales/521319/

Gregg, Melissa. *Counterproductive: Time Management in the Knowledge Economy*. Durham: Duke University Press, 2018.

Grimm, Jacob, and Wilhelm Grimm. *Briefwechsel zwischen Jacob und Wilhelm Grimm aus Der Jugendzeit*. [Correspondence Between Jacob and Wilhelm Grimm from Their Youth]. 2nd ed. Edited by Herman Grimm and Gustav Hinrichs. Weimar: Hermann Böhlaus Nachfolger, 1963.

——. 'Aschenputtel.' In *The Original Folk and Fairy Tales of the Brothers Grimm: The Complete First Edition*. Translated by Jack Zipes, 69-77. Princeton: Princeton University Press, 2014.

——. 'Hans My Hedgehog.' In *The Original Folk and Fairy Tales of the Brothers Grimm: The Complete First Edition*. Translated by Jack Zipes, 354-359. Princeton: Princeton University Press, 2014.

——. 'Old Sultan.' In *The Complete Fairy Tales of the Brothers Grimm All-New Third Edition*. Translated by Jack Zipes, 166-168. New York: Bantam, 2003. [From the 7th and final edition of the original German publication.]

——. 'Rapunzel.' In *The Complete Fairy Tales of the Brothers Grimm All-New Third Edition*. Translated by Jack Zipes, 43-45. New York: Bantam Books, 2003. [From the 7th and final edition of the original German publication.]

——. 'Rapunzel.' In *The Original Folk and Fairy Tales of the Brothers Grimm: The Complete First Edition*. Translated by Jack Zipes, 37-39. Princeton: Princeton University Press, 2014.

——. 'Simple Hans.' In *The Original Folk and Fairy Tales of the Brothers Grimm: The Complete First Edition*. Translated by Jack Zipes, 178-181. Princeton: Princeton University Press, 2014.

——. 'Snow White.' In *The Original Folk and Fairy Tales of the Brothers Grimm: The Complete First Edition*. Translated by Jack Zipes, 170-178. Princeton: Princeton University Press, 2014.

——. 'The Two Travellers.' *The Complete Fairy Tales of the Brothers Grimm All-New Third Edition*. Translated by Jack Zipes, 353-360. New York: Bantam, 2003. [From the 7th and final edition of the original German publication.]

Gurza, Andrew. 'I Told My Mom I Hire Sex Workers And Her Response Changed Our Relationship.' *HuffPost*, April 3, 2019. https://www.huffpost.com/entry/disability-sex-workers_n_5ca21581e4b00ba6328062d8

——. 'Sex, Pleasure, and Disability.' Girl Boner Radio. Podcast audio, May 4, 2019. podcasts.apple.com/us/podcast/sex-pleasure-and-disability/id814715884?i=1000437211012

Habermeyer, Ryan. 'William Osler, Medicine, and Fairy Tales.' Fugitive Leaves (blog). The Historical Medical Library of The College of Physicians of Philadelphia, January 9, 2019. histmed.collegeofphysicians.org/ osler-medicine-fairy-tales/

Hayes, Chris. 'The idea that the moral universe inherently bends towards justice is inspiring. It's also wrong.' Think: Opinion, Analysis, Essays (blog). NBC News Digital, March 24, 2018. www.nbcnews.com/think/opinion/idea-moral-universe-inherently-bends-towards-justice-inspiring-it-s-ncna859661

Hiskey, Daven. 'Sleeping Beauty is Based on a Story Where a Married King Finds a Girl Asleep and Can't Wake Her, So Rapes Her Instead'. Todayifoundout.com. October 29, 2012. www.todayifoundout.com/ index.php/2012/10/sleeping-beauty-is-based-on-a-story-where-a-married-king-finds-a-girl-asleep-and-cant-wake-her-so-rapes-her-instead/

Hudec, Mariah. 'Changelings and Sexual Coercion: Trauma and the Nature of Fairy Belief and Spirit-guide Relationships in Early Modern Scotland.' Master's Thesis, University of Edinburgh, 2014. www.academia.edu/10033810/Changelings_and_Sexual_Coercion_Trauma_and_the_Nature_of_Fairy_Belief_and_Spirit-guide_Relationships_in_Early_Modern_Scotland

Humphreys, Robin. Consult notes, March 1987.

Jane, J. S., T. F. Oltmanns, S. C. South, and E. Turkheimer. 'Gender bias in diagnostic criteria for personality disorders: an item response theory analysis.' Abstract. *Journal of Abnormal Psychology* 116, no. 1 (February 2007): 166-75. www.ncbi.nlm.nih.gov/pubmed/17324027

Johnson, Erica. 'Bell's 'Let's Talk' campaign rings hollow for employees suffering panic attacks, vomiting and anxiety.' CBC News, November 25, 2017. www.cbc.ca/news/health/bell-employees-stressed-by-sales-targets-1.4418876

Kamenetsky, Christa. 'The German Folklore Revival in the Eighteenth Century: Herder's Theory of Naturpoesie.' *The Journal of Popular Culture* 6, no. 4 (Spring 1973): 836-848. https://onlinelibrary.wiley.com/doi/abs/10.1111/j.0022-3840.1973.00836.x

Kay, Molly. '"Peppa Pig" Introducing Mandy Mouse Is a Major Moment for Disability Representation.' *Teen Vogue,* May 30, 2019. https://www.teenvogue.com/story/peppa-pig-mandy-mouse-disability-representation

Kim, Sarah. 'Ali Stroker's Tony Award Was Only Broadway's First Step To Disability Inclusivity.' Forbes.com. Jone 13, 2019. www.forbes.com/sites/sarahkim/2019/06/13/ali-stroker-tony-award/#763b504c7a73

Klein, Betsy, and Kevin Liptak. 'Trump ramps up rhetoric: Dems want "illegal immigrants" to "infest our country."' CNN, June 19, 2018. www. cnn.com/2018/06/19/politics/trump-illegal-immigrants-infest/ index.html

Kofoid, Jessica. 'Walking in High Heels: The Physics Behind the Physique.' *Illumin: A Review of Engineering in Everyday Life* 2, no. 8 (September 2007). illumin.usc.edu/walking-in-high-heels-the-physics-behind-the-physique/

Konstan, David. 'Beauty, Love and Art: The Legacy of Ancient Greece.' ΣΧΟΛΗ: *Ancient Philosophy and the Classical Tradition* 7, no. 2 (June 2013):

325-337. pdfs.semanticscholar.org/3c4f/87a03df2fb1bf9b670fbf3232b950a985cdd.pdf

Ladau, Emily. 'Why Person-First Language Doesn't Always Put the Person First.' *Think Inclusive*, July 20, 2015. www.thinkinclusive.us/why-person-first-language-doesnt-always-put-the-person-first/

Lapointe, Grace. 'Ambulatory: How the Little Mermaid Shaped My Self-Image with Cerebral Palsy.' *Monstering*, March 28, 2018. www.monstering-mag.com/blog/2018/3/28/ambulatory-how-the-little-mermaid-shaped-my-self-image-with-cerebral-palsy

Leprince du Beaumont, Jeanne-Marie. 'Beauty and the Beast.' *The Young Misses Magazine, Containing Dialogues between a Governess and Several Young Ladies of Quality Her Scholars* 4th ed., no. 1 (1783), 45-67. Accessed January 2, 2019, on Folklore and Mythology Electronic Texts. www.pitt.edu/~dash/beauty.html

Lewis, Talila A. 'Longmore Lecture: Context, Clarity, and Grounding.' Academic blog. March 5, 2019. Accessed October 25, 2019. www.talilalewis.com/blog.

Liddle, Siân. 'Despite appearances, not all people with scarred faces are movie villains.' *The Conversation Canada*, October 19, 2017. theconversation.com/despite-appearances-not-all-people-with-scarred-faces-are-movie-villains-84732

Lindahl, Carl. 'Jacks: The Name, The Tales, The American Traditions.' In *Jack In Two Worlds*, edited by William Bernard McCarthy, pp. xiii-xxxiv. Chapel Hill: University of North Carolina Press, 1994. www.folkstreams.net/film-context.php?id=258

Lombroso, Cesare. 'Left-Handedness and Left-Sidedness.' *The North American Review* 177, no. 562 (September 1903): 440-444. Accessed February 18, 2019, on JSTOR. www.jstor.org/stable/25119452?origin=JSTOR-pdf

Lowe, Johannes. 'British Film Institute says it will no longer fund films which star villains with facial scarring'. *The Telegraph*. November 27, 2018. www.telegraph.co.uk/news/2018/11/27/british-film-institute-says-will-no-longer-fund-films-star-villains/

Lyons, Kate. '"Here is a story! Story it is": how fairytales are told in other tongues.' *The Guardian*, April 19, 2019. www.theguardian.com/books/2019/apr/19/here-is-a-story-story-it-is-how-fairytales-are-told-in-other-tongues

Markus, Christopher, and Stephen McFeely. *Captain America: The First Avenger*. Streaming Video. Directed by Joe Johnston. Hollywood: Paramount Pictures, 2011.

Merriam-Webster Online Dictionary, s.v. 'ableism', accessed January 14, 2019, www.merriam-webster.com/dictionary/ableism

McBryde Johnson, Harriet. *Too Late To Die Young*. New York: Picador, 2006.

McCarthy, Michael J. F. *Five Years in Ireland, 1895-1900*. Dublin: Hodges, Figgis & Co., Ltd., 1901. Accessed February 6, 2019, on Library Ireland. www.libraryireland.com/articles/Burning-Bridget-Cleary/index.php

Min, Sarah. 'Social Security may use your Facebook and Instagram photos to nix disability claims.' CBS News, March 21, 2019. www. cbsnews.com/ news/social-security-disability-benefits-your-facebook-instagram-posts-could-affect-your-social-security-disability-claim/

Mitchell, David T., and Sharon L. Snyder. *Narrative Prosthesis: Disability and the Dependencies of Discourse*. Ann Arbor: University of Michigan Press, 2001.

Munsch, Robert. *The Paper Bag Princess*. Illustrated by Michael Martchenko. Toronto: Annick Press, 1980.

O'Farrell, Maggie. *I Am, I Am, I Am: Seventeen Brushes With Death*. Toronto: Knopf Canada, 2018.

Oliver, Michael, and Bob Sapey. *Social Work with Disabled People*. 3rd ed. Basingstoke: Palgrave Macmillan, 2006.

Oring, Elliott, and Steven Swann Jones. 'On the Meanings of Mother Goose.' *Western Folklore* 46, no. 2 (April 1987): 106-114. Accessed June 27, 2019, on JSTOR. www.jstor.org/stable/1499928

Owens, Janine. 'Exploring the critiques of the social model of disability: the transformative possibility of Arendt's notion of power.' *Sociology of Health & Illness* 37, no. 3 (March 2015): 385-403. onlinelibrary.wiley.com/ doi/full/10.1111/1467-9566.12199

Pérez Cuervo, Maria J. 'The Bizarre Death of Bridget Cleary, the Irish 'Fairy Wife'.' *Mental Floss*, April 17, 2018. mentalfloss.com/article/539793/ bizarre-death-bridget-cleary-irish-fairy-wife

Perrault, Charles. 'Cinderella; or, The Little Glass Slipper.' In *The Blue Fairy Book*, edited by Andrew Lang, 64-71. London: Longmans, Green, and Co., ca. 1889. Accessed February 17, 2019, on Folklore and Mythology Electronic Texts. www.pitt.edu/~dash/perrault06.html

Perrault, Charles. 'Ricky of the Tuft.' In *Old-Time Stories told by Master Charles Perrault*, translated by A. E. Johnson. New York: Dodd Mead and Company, 1921. Accessed February 8, 2019, on Folklore and Mythology Electronic Texts. www.pitt.edu/~dash/perrault07.html

———. 'Sleeping Beauty.' In *Old-Time Stories told by Master Charles Perrault*, translated by A. E. Johnson. New York: Dodd Mead and Company, 1921. Accessed December 8, 2018, on Folklore and Mythology Electronic Texts. www.pitt.edu/~dash/perrault01.html

———. *Old-Time Stories told by Master Charles Perrault*. Translated by A. E. Johnson. New York: Dodd Mead and Company, 1921. Accessed February 14, 2019, on Folklore and Mythology Electronic Texts. www.pitt.edu/ ~dash/perrault.html

Phillips, Brian. 'Once and Future Queen.' In *Impossible Owls: Essays*. New York: Farrar, Straus and Giroux, 2018.

Piepzna-Samarasinha, Leah Lakshmi. *Care Work: Dreaming Disability Justice*. Vancouver: Arsenal Pulp Press, 2018.

Pring, John. 'Action on Hearing Loss defends holding comedy fundraiser in inaccessible venue.' Disability News Service, May 9, 2019. www.disability

newsservice.com/action-on-hearing-loss-defends-holding-comedy-fundraiser-in-inaccessible-venue/

Propp, Vladimir. *Morphology of the Folktale*. 2nd ed. Translated by Laurence Scott. Austin: University of Texas Press, 1968.

———. *Theory and History of Folklore*. Translated by Ariadna Y. Martin and Richard P. Martin. Edited by Anatoly Liberman. Minneapolis: University of Minnesota Press, 1984.

Radin, Paul, ed. 'How Spider Obtained the Sky-God's Stories.' In *African Folktales*, 25-27. New York: Schocken Books, 1983.

Röhrich, Lutz. *Folktales and Reality*. Translated by Peter Tokofsky. Bloomington: Indiana University Press, 1991.

Romain, Lindsey. 'How Game of Thrones Failed Daenerys Targaryen.' Nerdist, May 14, 2019. nerdist.com/article/game-of-thrones-failed-daenerys-targaryen/

Roth, Melissa. *The Left Stuff: How the Left-Handed Have Survived and Thrived in a Right-Handed World*. Lanham: M. Evans and Company, 2009.

Schmiesing, Ann. *Disability, Deformity, and Disease in the Grimms' Fairy Tales*. Detroit: Wayne State University Press, 2014.

Siebers, Tobin. *Disability Aesthetics*. Ann Arbor: University of Michigan Press, 2010.

———. *Disability Theory*. Ann Arbor: University of Michigan Press, 2008.

smith, s. e., and Matthew Cortland. 'A Trump Proposal Could Make Selfies Dangerous for Disabled People.' TalkPoverty.org (blog). Center for American Progress, March 28, 2019. talkpoverty.org/2019/03/28/trump-selfies-dangerous-disabled-people/

Sontag, Susan. *Illness as Metaphor and AIDS and Its Metaphors*. New York: Picador, 2001.

Snow, Blake. 'The Science of High Heels: How Physics Keeps Women from Falling Down.' Fox News, last updated June 22, 2015. www.foxnews.com/science/the-science-of-high-heels-how-physics-keeps-women-from-falling-down

Squire, Michael. *The Art of the Body: Antiquity and Its Legacy*. Oxford: Oxford University Press, 2011.

Stark, Jill. 'Anxiety, depression and the "fairy tale filter."' Big Ideas, ABC Radio National. Podcast audio, August 8, 2018. www.abc.net.au/radionational/programs/bigideas/anxiety,-depression,-and-the-happiness-myth/10204250

Priestley, Mark. 'Fundamental Principles of Disability: Being a summary of the discussion held on 22nd November, 1975 and containing commentaries from each organization [The Union of the Physically Impaired Against Segregation and The Disability Alliance].' In consultation with Vic Finkelstein and Ken Davis. Disability Resource Centre, October 1997. www.disability.co.uk/sites/default/files/resources/fundamental%20principles.pdf

Thompson, Janet. 'The Folklore Tradition of Jack Tales.' 2004. ccb.lis.illinois. edu/Projects/storytelling/jsthomps/tales.htm. The Internet Archive: Wayback Machine. Last updated April 10, 2014. web.archive.org/web/20140410004237/http://ccb.lis.illinois.edu/Projects/storytelling/jsthomps/tales.htm

Thorne, Will. "Special's' Ryan O'Connell Talks Centering a TV Series on a Character with Cerebral Palsy.' *Variety*, April 5, 2019. variety.com/2019/tv/features/ryan-oconnell-special-disability-representation-interview-1203175586/

Tilton Ratcliff, Ace. 'As a Disabled Writer, I Know My Stories are Worth Telling.' *Catapult*, February 14, 2019. catapult.co/stories/fahrenheit-451-ray-bradbury-disability-writing-block-ace-tilton-ratcliff

Urquhart, Emily. *Beyond the Pale: Folklore, Family, and the Mystery of Our Hidden Genes*. Toronto: Harper Perennial, 2016.

Warner, Marina. *Once Upon A Time: A Short History of Fairy Tale*. Oxford: Oxford University Press, 2014.

Wikipedia. 'Disney Princess.' Last updated July 10, 2019, 01:37 (UTC). en.wikipedia.org/w/index.php?title=Disney_Princess&oldid=905584945

Wikipedia. 'Sense8.' Last updated July 8, 2019, 09:56 (UTC). en.wikipedia.org/w/index.php?title=Sense8&oldid=905313397

Willis McCullough, David. 'The Fairy Defense,' reviews of *The Burning of Bridget Cleary: A True Story*, by Angela Bourke, and *The Cooper's Wife is Missing: The Trials of Bridget Cleary*, by Joan Hoff and Marian Yeates. *The New York Times*, October 8, 2000. www.nytimes.com/2000/10/08/books/the-fairy-defense.html

Whaley, Kayla. '(Don't) Fear the Feeding Tube.' *Catapult*. May 8, 2018. Accessed October 25, 2019. catapult.co/stories/column-hard-to-swallow-dont-fear-the-feeding-tube

World Health Organization. 'Disabilities: Definition.' Accessed January 4, 2019. www.who.int/topics/disabilities/en/

Wong, Alice. 'Unbroken and Unbowed: Revisiting Disability Representation on "Game of Thrones."' *Bitch*, May 29, 2019. www.bitchmedia. org/article/game-of-thrones-disability-roundtable

Woolverton, Linda. Maleficent. DVD. Directed by Robert Stromberg. Burbank: Walt Disney Studios Motion Pictures, 2014.

Wynn, Debbi. 'A beauty beyond skin deep.' CNN, April 17, 2013. www.cnn.com/2013/04/14/health/loker-profile/index.html

Zipes, Jack. *Breaking the Magic Spell: Radical Theories of Folk & Fairy Tales*. Revised ed. edition. Lexington, University Press of Kentucky, 2002.

———. *The Oxford Companion to Fairy Tales*. Second Edition. Oxford: Oxford University Press, 2015.

———. *The Irresistible Fairy Tale: The Cultural and Social History of a Genre*. Princeton: Princeton University Press, 2013.

———. *When Dreams Came True: Classical Fairy Tales and Their Tradition*. 2nd ed. New York: Routledge, 2007.

Acknowledgements

Thanks as always to my agent, Samantha Haywood, for unwavering belief and cheer. To Alana Wilcox and Melanie Little for the wonderful, incisive edits; to Ricky Lima, James Lindsay, Crystal Sikma, and the rest of the team at Coach House Books for giving this book and this author such a lovely home.

I am deeply grateful to all of the members of the disability community who shared their stories and their lives with me in the course of writing *Disfigured*. Thank you to Tinu Abayomi-Paul, Natalie Abbott, Kelly Aiello, Madeleine Battista, Rebecca Cokley, Irené Colthurst, André Daughtry, Laura Dorwart, Dominick Evans, Jeannine Hall Gailey, Andrew Gurza, Sarah Jama, Errol Kerr, Bethany Killen, Jónina Kirton, Grace Lapointe, Cara Liebowitz, Penny Loker, Dominik Parisien, Adam Pottle, Elsa Sjunesson-Henry, Rebecca Thorne, Emily Urquhart, Jerome van Leeuwen, Allison Wallis, and David Williamson. I hope there is something in this book that speaks to you the way you've all spoken to and given hope to me.

The work of disability rights is a long and winding road. I am privileged to follow in the path of so many brilliant individuals and writers who have fought this fight for so long. Thank you in particular to Imani Barbarin (#HashtagQueen), Bronwyn Berg, Patty Berne, Keah Brown, Hamilton, Mia Mingus, Mike Oliver, Dorothy Ellen Palmer, Leah Lakshmi Piepzna-Samarasinha, Vilissa Thompson, Ace Tilton-Ratcliff, Alice Wong, and Stella Young. Your fierceness and love have carried so many of us, and I will be forever grateful.

Many thanks to Sarah Henstra for sitting down to talk fairy tales and the hostile world; to Pauline Greenhill at the

University of Winnipeg for her stellar advice and recommendations; and to Tea Gerbeza for her wonderful thesis on ableism in the *Harry Potter* books.

Heartfelt thanks to Garnette Cadogan and Jonny Diamond, who were instrumental in shaping Chapter Eight, 'Monsters and Marvels,' and giving it its first home as a standalone piece at LitHub.

I am indebted to Shay Erlich for their careful read of this book, and for helping to ensure that I was as open and sensitive in the work as I could be.

Many thanks to the Ontario Arts Council and the Canada Council for the Arts, whose financial support made the completion of this book possible. Thanks also to the Ontario Heritage Trust and the Doris McCarthy Artist-in-Residence program, for providing the space and quiet necessary for *Disfigured* to come alive.

Thanks to Jess Babcock, Harolynne Bobis, Amy Fournier, Vito Zingarelli, and everyone else at Hedgebrook who continue to create and nurture space for women authors and their stories.

Thanks to the friends who remind me that one is never alone in this writing business: Carleigh Baker, Trevor Cole, Sean Cranbury, Jessica Desanta, Liz Harmer, Jaime Krakowski, Jen Sookfong Lee, Adam Pottle, Ben Rawluk, Amanda Reaume, Jael Richardson, Peter Snow, Sarah Taggart, and Andrew Wilmot.

Special witchy coven thanks to Piyali Bhattacharya, Vero González, Mira Jacob, Ashley M. Jones, Lisa Nikolidakis, and Yaccaira Salvatierra, who were there with me at Hedgebrook when the idea for this book came into being. Our friendship is the stuff of magic, and I will always be grateful that the world brought us together.

Thanks to my family – Raymond and Debra Leduc, Alex Leduc, Aimee Leduc, and Allison, Adam, Areyana, and Adelyn DiFilippo – for believing in me always.

Finally – thank you to Sitka, the Dog of Doom, who saw fit to not tear this manuscript apart, for which I am very grateful.

About the Author

Amanda Leduc's essays and stories have appeared in publications across Canada, the US, and the UK. She is the author of the novels *The Miracles of Ordinary Men* and the forthcoming *The Centaur's Wife*. She has cerebral palsy and lives in Hamilton, Ontario, where she works as the Communications Coordinator for the Festival of Literary Diversity (FOLD), Canada's first festival for diverse authors and stories.

Other Exploded Views Titles

Typeset in Aldus Nova and Gibson Pro.

Printed at the Coach House on bpNichol Lane in Toronto, Ontario, on Rolland Natural paper, which was manufactured, acid-free, in Saint-Jérôme, Quebec, from 30 per cent recycled paper. This book was printed with vegetable-based ink on a 1973 Heidelberg KORD offset litho press. Its pages were folded on a Baumfolder, gathered by hand, bound on a Sulby Auto-Minabinda, and trimmed on a Polar single-knife cutter.

Coach House is located on the traditional territory of many nations, including the Mississaugas of the Credit, the Anishnaabeg, the Haudenosaunee, the Chippewa, and the Wendat peoples, and is now home to many diverse First Nations, Métis, and Inuit people. Toronto is covered by Treaty 13 signed with the Mississaugas of the Credit, and the Williams Treaties signed with multiple Mississaugas and Chippewa bands. We are grateful to live and work on this land.

Seen through the press by Alana Wilcox
Edited by Melanie Little
Cover illustration by Chloe Cushman
Author photo by Trevor Cole
Cover design and series template designed by Ingrid Paulson

Coach House Books
80 bpNichol Lane
Toronto ON M5S 3J4
Canada

416 979 2217
800 367 6360

mail@chbooks.com
www.chbooks.com